Ann Miller
TOPS IN TAPS

Ann Miller
TOPS IN TAPS
An Authorized Pictorial History.

By
JIM CONNOR

AUTHOR OF
HOLLYWOOD STARLET: THE CAREER
OF BARBARA LAWRENCE

With an
Introduction by
HERMES PAN

A GROLIER COMPANY

FRANKLIN WATTS
NEW YORK | LONDON | TORONTO | SYDNEY
1981

FOR MAMA KAT

The idea for this book was from Jeff Parker. I am indebted to him not only for making his extensive collection of Ann Miller memorabilia available to me but also his support for the project. My thanks also to my agent, George Ziegler, for his optimism and enthusiasm. Emily Garlin copyedited the manuscript with a keen eye, and she has my admiration. For their editorial help, a round of applause goes to Carol Houck Smith, Sherry Huber, Iva Ashner, Robert Osborne, and Paula Kramer and Ira Kramer of *Movie Star News*. And Richard Gingrich. Last, to Bob Levine of Franklin Watts, Inc. my gratitude for making the project happen.

The photographs used in this book are from Parker's collection and from my private collection, with thanks to the motion picture studios, RKO Radio, Republic, Columbia, Paramount, and Metro-Goldwyn-Mayer, who were responsible for the musicals and comedies of Ann Miller.

Sugar Babies photographs courtesy of Martha Swope and reprinted by permission.

Book design by Nick Krenitsky

Library of Congress Cataloging in Publication Data

Connor, Jim
Ann Miller, tops in taps.

1. Miller, Ann, 1923-   . I. Title.
PN2287.M635C6   793.3'2'0924   80-28191
ISBN 0-531-09949-0
ISBN 0-531-09950-4 (pbk.)

Jacket photograph copyright © by Martha Swope

Caricature on page 2 copyright © by
Al Hirschfeld. Used by permission.

Photograph on page 224 by Bill King.
Used by permission of Peter Rogers Associates.

Hermes Pan choreographing a routine for Ann
for *Radio City Revels*.

Introduction

BY HERMES PAN

The first time I met Ann was at RKO in the '30s when I was working on *Radio City Revels*. I was also her first Hollywood date, and I thought she was eighteen. She was only fourteen! (She had lied about her age to get a movie contract.) When I went to pick her up at her apartment, her mother greeted me. "Ann will be right out. Sit down and have yourself a snort," she said in an accent from deep in the heart of Texas. When Ann came in I was glad that I'd had the snort. It prepared me for what I saw. She could have been Claudette Colbert or Theda Bara made up for their roles in *Cleopatra*.

I asked her mother to make her wash her face before we went out. Ann complied and returned a little more subdued, but her face still looked like the death mask of Nefertiti.

Not many people know the real Ann Miller. This fact was highlighted to me recently at the unveiling of a painting of her by a prominent portrait artist, at a small party I gave for the occasion. When the covering was drawn aside a surprised, bewildered quiet settled over the select group present. The almost life-size portrait showed a serious-faced Ann. Her hair was pulled back severely and parted down the middle, and she had an almost sad, wistful expression. No wig, no jewelry, no false eyelashes, no furs, no frills—not the Ann Miller people think of.

When the surprise had subsided and friends had given their comments, compliments, etc., Ann walked over and stood beside the painting and said, "Believe it or not, this is the *real* Ann Miller."

I later heard that she persuaded the artist to touch up the portrait by adding a few baubles, a little more blue eyeshadow, longer lashes, and more lipstick! Symbolic? People had seen enough of the real Ann.

Being a star is a commitment to Ann; she feels she owes the public an obligation to show them what they want, and expect, a star to look and act like. There's no "girl next door," "cutie in the kitchen," "shirt-tale out and faded jeans" image in her life-style. She is the true product of the Golden Era of Hollywood—an era of glamour, illusion, and escapism.

Paradoxically, Ann is as unaffected, simple, loyal, honest, and out-spoken as the free windswept plains of her Texas heritage.

In Hollywood, Ann's "Millerisms"—as they have become known—are legendary; not since Sam Goldwyn has anyone been so quoted and misquoted on remarks made on various and sundry occasions. For example, she once said to a deposed and exiled ex-queen, a victim of international political upheavals and personal tragedies, "Your Majesty, if you think you've got troubles, I just broke my toe!" This was not an attempt to be funny, witty, or rude. It was just Ann's way of showing empathy, to console and express affinity with her royal acquaintance. After all, breaking a toe for Ann was indeed a major tragedy.

It is strange that in her many films and Hollywood career, no studio or producer ever really captured, exploited, or understood the full potential of Ann's many talents. Maybe the mask of Nefertiti was hiding too much of the real Ann Miller.

Now she is the superstar that she should have been years ago. A Latin axiom—*The higher the organism the slower the development*—seems to be the case with Ann.

Ann the Honest. Ann the Flashy. Ann the Mystic. Ann the Sad. Will the real Ann Miller please stand up?

I haven't said anything about her dancing, because it needs no comment. As her choreographer for many years, I can only say she is simply one of the greatest tap dancers in the world. Fortunately, her performances are preserved on film and I believe posterity will be the richer for it.

The name HERMES PAN is synonymous with the finest dances in the best musical films of Hollywood's Golden Age. Pan has been associated with Fred Astaire throughout his motion picture career (*The Gay Divorcee, Top Hat, Shall We Dance?*, and *The Barkleys of Broadway*, among others). Pan won an Oscar in 1937 for his choreography of the "Fun House Number" in RKO's *A Damsel in Distress*, and an Emmy for his choreography for the television special, "An Evening with Fred Astaire." He created the routines for Betty Grable's Twentieth Century-Fox musicals and appeared with her in such films as *Pin-Up Girl, Sweet Rosie O'Grady*, and *Moon Over Miami*. At M-G-M, Pan choreographed *Jupiter's Darling, Meet Me in Las Vegas, Silk Stockings*, and many others. His contemporary work includes *Porgy and Bess, Can-Can, My Fair Lady, Finian's Rainbow*, and *Darling Lili*. Most recently, Pan received the "Achievement in Cinema" award from the National Film Society. Pan's association with Ann Miller began at RKO in *Radio City Revels* and *Stage Door*, and continued at M-G-M with such films as *Texas Carnival, Lovely to Look At*, and *Kiss Me Kate*.

THE RKO YEARS

The motion picture shooting on the Grand National lot in 1936 was *The Devil on Horseback*, a relatively unimportant programmer. The star was Lili Damita, an actress best remembered as Errol Flynn's first wife. One of the chorus girls, Johnnie Lucille Collier, had already appeared before the cameras as a child extra in *Anne of Green Gables* (which gave Anne Shirley her name) and *The Good Fairy* (which starred Margaret Sullavan), but in *The Devil on Horseback* Johnnie Lucille made her dancing debut—not very auspicious, but nonetheless a start for the young girl who would soon be known to movie audiences as Ann Miller.

Johnnie Lucille and her mother, Clara Collier, came to Hollywood from Texas, impelled by the dream that Johnnie Lucille would become a dancing star. In the 1930's, that dream was a common one shared by many hopeful young girls and their mothers.

Johnnie Lucille Collier was born in Houston, Texas, on April 12, 1923. Her mother was stage-struck and enrolled her daughter in dancing school when she was three years old. They saw all the movie musicals and vaudeville acts that appeared in Houston. Johnnie Lucille was a good student and took easily to tap dancing. Soon she was dancing

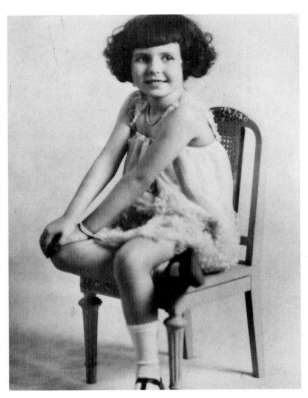

Johnnie Lucille Collier—
four years old.

at local functions—women's organizations, the Big Brother's Club in
Houston—and gaining a regional dance reputation.

When Johnnie Lucille was eleven, Clara and her husband, Texas
lawyer John Alfred Collier, separated and then divorced. Clara was faced
with raising her child alone.

The two returned to California, where they had vacationed only a
few months earlier, so Clara could concentrate on her dream of making her daughter a dancing star. Johnnie Lucille had attended dancing
school and had done extra work in the movies during their vacation. In
those days, Texas made no provision for alimony. Now little Johnnie
Lucille had to earn money to support herself and her mother from the
few dance routines that she knew as her mother was deaf and couldn't
hold a job. Work was not plentiful in California, especially for an
under-age dancer. But they survived.

Johnnie Lucille Collier was certainly not a perfect stage name.
Harry Fields, a pianist who played theater and club dates, such as the
Lions Club and the Rotary Club, for the young dancer, suggested that
she change it to something simple and easy to remember like *Anne
Miller*—with an "e" on Ann.

A contest at the Orpheum Theater in Los Angeles promised five
dollars to each entrant. The winner would get a two-week engagement
at the theater at fifty dollars per week. Johnnie Lucille Collier, now
known as Anne Miller, won the contest. She was billed as a "tap dancer

with a new style." The manager of the Orpheum Theater, Sherrill C. Corwin, is now Hollywood's biggest theater owner and producer.

A year passed and Anne Miller was still no nearer to featured parts in the movies than as a long-legged chorus dancer in *The Devil on Horseback* in high heels and bust pads. At this time she was offered a three-week contract at the famous Bal Tabarin Club in San Francisco. Anne Miller and her mother reluctantly left Hollywood and their movie dreams to fulfill the engagement. The thirteen-year-old dancer was now earning one hundred dollars a week. She was held over for sixteen weeks, creating new tap routines every four weeks, and was a smash hit.

During the Bal Tabarin engagement, Lucille Ball, who was then an RKO starlet, and Benny Rubin, a talent scout for the studio, saw Anne dance. Lucille Ball thought she might be movie material, and Rubin arranged for a screen test. The test was directed by William Grady and it resulted in RKO Radio Pictures signing Ann Miller (and dropping the *e* from her name) at $150 per week thinking she was an adult.

To avoid any confusion, Clara Collier became Clara Miller. Ann's father arranged for a phony birth certificate so that Ann appeared to be eighteen years old. Her name on this birth certificate was Lucy Ann Collier (in honor of Lucille Ball and Ann's new name), and Chireno, Texas, the home of her grandparents, was listed as her place of birth. Clara felt the studio heads would be ill-disposed toward their new dis-

**A chorus number from *Devil on Horseback*.
Ann is in the front row, center left.**

covery if they knew she was only thirteen years old, so five years were added to Ann's age. Since Ann was tall for her age the deception worked, and RKO promptly featured their new contract player tap dancing one number in *New Faces of 1937*.

Audience reaction to Ann's tap dancing in *New Faces of 1937* was positive.[1] The movie spotlighted many new performers, but Ann was the only one who created a lasting impact even though she had only one number to do in the film. Audience reaction guided the studios and was taken very seriously.

RKO quickly followed up Ann's success with another dance sequence in *The Life of the Party*. This time she was given two numbers to perform and received featured billing along with comic "sneezer" Billy Gilbert.

The critics were quick to compare Ann's tap dancing with that of Eleanor Powell, who was then the reigning dancing star of the opulent Metro-Goldwyn-Mayer musicals. *Variety* reported that even the military costume Ann wore in the "Doodle Band" number was too similar to Miss Powell's finale costume of *Broadway Melody of 1937*. At this time, Ann was earning only $150 per week doing machine gun taps at RKO while M-G-M was paying Miss Powell $250,000 per picture.

In *Stage Door*, Ann got her chance to say a few lines and to be the dance partner of Ginger Rogers. Hermes Pan choreographed their nightclub number, "Put Your Heart into Your Feet and Dance." Ann held her own with the seasoned professional cast, which included her discoverer, Lucille Ball. The film version of the Kaufman and Ferber stage play was a financial and critical hit.

RKO wasted no time in promoting their new dancing personality. She was promptly elevated to star billing in *Radio City Revels*, her fourth movie, which co-starred Bob Burns, Jack Oakie, and Kenny Baker. Not bad for a youngster of fourteen. Ironically, *Variety* now reported: "Miss Miller is a right smart tapster on the Eleanor Powell order." Kenny Baker gave Ann her first screen kiss in *Radio City Revels*. Hermes Pan, again Ann's choreographer, was also Ann's first real date. He escorted her to the 1938 Academy Awards ceremony. Magazine articles appeared and publicity was churned out for movie fans wanting to know about this rising new Hollywood dancer with the long legs who became the world's fastest tap dancer according to Ripley's "Believe It or Not" who, by attaching a speedometer to her feet as she danced, noted 500 taps per minute.

Having Wonderful Time was Ann's next movie in theatrical release, although *You Can't Take It with You* was filmed first.

Largely because of Ann's success in *Radio City Revels*, Columbia Pictures managed to borrow her from RKO for the role of the dizzy ballerina, Essie Carmichael, in Frank Capra's production of *You Can't Take It with You*. Ann was not a ballet dancer and had to take some

1. In a *Look* magazine article dated January 14, 1941, choreographer Hermes Pan remembered seeing Ann rehearsing for *New Faces of 1937* and remarking, "It's a lie. Nobody can tap that fast."

At the time Ann signed her contract
with RKO-Radio Pictures.

hurried instruction from dance teacher Ada Broadbent. Essie was supposed to be a mediocre ballet dancer, so the pain of being "sur les pointes" only helped Ann's characterization, and the prestige of being cast in a Frank Capra picture more than compensated for having to stuff her feet into toe shoes and twirl on her toes.

Columbia had bought the movie rights to the Kaufman and Hart Pulitzer Prize-winning play for $200,000—a staggering price during the depression of the 1930's. *You Can't Take It with You* won the Academy Award for Best Picture of 1938.

The studio also sent Ann on her first nationwide personal appearance tour with this hit movie. She appeared in as many as six or eight shows a day as the star of a stage show in theaters where the movie was playing. It is interesting to note that newcomer Richard "Red" Skelton, who was just at the beginning of his career, was last-billed on theater marquees where Ann was starred.

Back from tour, Ann reported for work at her home studio, RKO. The film version of Arthur Kober's play *Having Wonderful Time,* which starred Ginger Rogers and Douglas Fairbanks, Jr., did nothing to further Ann's career. She did have featured billing, along with screen newcomer Richard "Red" Skelton, but Ann's scenes were cut from the film. In the finished print it is difficult even to spot Ann in the crowd scenes. Hollywood eliminated the Jewish aspect of Kober's play, and with it its charm and social comment. The result was a tedious, obvious comedy.

Then RKO cast Ann as the love interest, opposite Frank Albertson, in *Room Service*, possibly the least successful of any of the Marx Brothers' films. Both Ann and Lucille Ball were virtually wasted in their roles. RKO didn't seem to know, or even to care, how to showcase their new dancing star. Ann landed at the bottom of the movie heap in a flop called *Tarnished Angel*. Even though she sang but didn't do a tap number in this melodrama starring Sally Eilers, and was singled out with good reviews, *Tarnished Angel* played theaters by filling in the second-feature slot. Ann's salary at this time was only $250 per week.

Ann's movie career was at a standstill. The William Morris Office asked for her release.

At this point, her agents, Johnny Hyde and Abe Lastfogel, of the William Morris Agency convinced Ann and her mother that a hit Broad-

Dance director Ada Broadbent limbers up Ann for ballet work in *You Can't Take It with You*.

way show would boost Ann's flagging movie career. *George White's Scandals* (see "Theater," below) proved to be a very wise career move for the fifteen-year-old dancer. The show was a huge hit at the Alvin Theater in New York, and for one year on the road. It did, indeed, revive movie interest in Ann Miller. RKO offered her $3,000 a week to star in the film version of *Too Many Girls*.

In a newspaper interview dated July 9, 1940, Ann said:

"The curtain hardly had fallen before the movie studios were in with bids for me to work in Hollywood, where, six months before, nobody had anything for me to do. The highest bid was from RKO to play in George Abbott's *Too Many Girls*.

"So I came on out here and went into the show sight unseen and it looks like history, insofar as Ann Miller is concerned, is about to repeat itself.

"Here they've given me that fancy salary and third billing and a star dressing room and I don't have more than a dozen lines to say in the whole film. All I do is dance.

"It seems sort of strange, after all that build-up. Yet I'm still grateful to RKO. In spite of what happened, I feel that everybody's been swell and I've still got high hopes."

Desi Arnaz recreated his original stage role in *Too Many Girls*. He played the bongos for Ann's lightning taps in the "Spic 'n' Spanish" number, and romanced Lucille Ball off-screen. *Too Many Girls* was a hit, and Ann Miller, at seventeen, had made a Hollywood comeback.

A Republic picture, *Hit Parade of 1941*, which was made after, but released before, *Too Many Girls*, reunited Ann with Kenny Baker, who had given her her first screen kiss in *Radio City Revels*. Her dancing scored high with the critics in this elaborate and expensive Republic musical. The *Hollywood Reporter* stated: "The beauty, brilliance and consummate grace of her artistry is an endless delight." (Whenever *Hit Parade of 1941* is shown on television today, it is entitled *Romance and Rhythm*.)

Gene Autry was Republic Pictures' leading cowboy star. In *Melody Ranch*, an ambitious $500,000 western production, Ann was cast as Autry's leading lady. Comedian Jimmy Durante was co-starred in this movie which Republic hoped would appeal to the non-regular Autry movie customers. Durante's fame would come later in many popular Metro-Goldwyn-Mayer movie musicals in the mid-1940's and on television.

In *Melody Ranch*, Ann was the first girl to be kissed in a movie by Gene Autry. But both Republic and Autry feared the displeasure of the cowboy star's loyal fans, and the camera cut away from Ann and Autry as they puckered up. The kiss was never seen on the screen.

Ann's movie career was again on the ascendant. Her next freelance assignment, starring in Columbia Pictures' *Time Out for Rhythm* (which won her a six-year contract with that studio), proved to be another important career move. Ann Miller now had a secure niche in Hollywood's musical films where she became the toast of servicemen during World War II and made Columbia Pictures a fortune. At this time Ann rivaled Columbia's crown princess, Rita Hayworth.

NEW FACES *of* **1937**

Release date: July 2, 1937

CAST

Seymore Seymore . . . . JOE PENNER
Wellington Wedge . . . . MILTON BERLE
Parky . . . . PARKYAKARKUS
Patricia . . . . HARRIET HILLIARD
Jimmy . . . . WILLIAM BRADY
Robert Hunt . . . . JEROME COWAN
Elaine . . . . THELMA LEEDS
Judge Hugo Straight . . . . Tommy Mack
Suzy . . . . Lorraine Krueger
Count Mischa Moody . . . . Bert Gordon
Hunt's secretary . . . . Patricia Wilder

Broker	Richard Lane
Stagemanager	Dudley Clements
Assistant stagemanager	William Corson
Doorman	George Rosener
Bridge guard	Harry Bernard
Joe Guzzola	Dewey Robinson
Count Moody's secretary	Harry C. Bradley

And: 100 NEW FACES

Specialties

Lowe, Hite and Stanley, Brian Sisters, Derry Dean, Eddie Rio and Bros., Seven Loria Bros., Catherine Brent, *Ann Miller*, Three Chocolateers, Four Playboys, Dorothy Roberts, Camille Soray, Rene Stone, Diane Toy.

CREDITS

Director: Leigh Jason *Producer:* Edward Small *Screenplay:* Nat Perrin, Philip G. Epstein, Irv S. Brecher *Adaptation:* Harold Kussell, Harry Clork, Howard J. Green *Based on the story Shoestring:* George Bradshaw *Sketch "A Day at the Brokers" by:* David Freedman *Musical director:* Roy Webb *Dance director:* Sammy Lee *Director of photography:* J. Roy Hunt *Special effects:* V. L. Walker *Film editor:* George Crone *Running time:* 105 minutes.

SONGS

Music and lyrics: Lew Brown, Sammy Fain, Walter Bullock, Harold Spina, Ben Pollack, Harry James, *additional lyrics:* Edward Cherkose, Charles Henderson, Joe Penner, Hal Raynor. "Peckin'," "Love Is Never Out of Season," "Penthouse on Third Avenue," "It Goes to Your Feet," "If I Didn't Have You," "New Faces of 1937," "Widow in Lace," "When the Berry Blossoms Bloom."

SYNOPSIS

Robert Hunt (Jerome Cowan), along with his stooge, Parky (Parkyakarkus), is a crooked Broadway producer. His scam is getting four backers for a show—like Wellington Wedge (Milton Berle)—selling each one 85 per cent, then pocketing the money when the show flops. *Revels*, his current show, folds.

Jimmy (William Brady), a bit player in *Revels*, and chorus girl Patricia (Harriet Hilliard) are in love, but Jimmy refuses to marry her until he can sell his play *New Faces*.

Patricia has inherited fifteen thousand dollars. She gives the money to Hunt to produce Jimmy's show, stipulating that he must not know her part in the production. Hunt immediately resumes his unscrupulous tactics—hiring bad acts and dismissing the good ones.

Elaine (Thelma Leeds), a dancer Hunt had dropped from *Revels*, tells Hunt she is on to his game. To keep her quiet he quickly proposes to her and throws in a trip to Europe. Wedge takes full charge of *New Faces*.

When Elaine discovers Hunt has tricked her, she tells Wedge he will face prosecution if the show is a hit. So Wedge decides to follow Hunt's practice of hiring bad material to make the show a flop.

En route to Atlantic City for the show's try-out, Patricia pleads with Wedge to save the show. Since Wedge is in love with her, he has a change of heart. Patricia kisses him. Jimmy sees this and gets the wrong idea.

On opening night, Seymore Seymore (Joe Penner), one of the bad acts, is fired again. But during the show he bursts through the curtain, does his act, and is sensational. *New Faces* is a hit. Jimmy then learns that Patricia is a backer and the reason Wedge tried to ruin the show. The backers are offered a four-way split, Wedge stays on as the show's manager, and Jimmy and Patricia can finally be married.

CRITICAL REACTION

Variety:

"All about a Broadway show, *New Faces of 1937* is the excuse for the marathon audition of talent. And, of course, the actual premiere of the show, for the finish, is another parade of new people. . . . As with many films of this type, it really reminds of a big short, held together by stray strands of plot. . . . Ann Miller doing good taps that drew a salvo at this screening."

Howard Barnes in the New York Herald Tribune:

"*New Faces of 1937* has almost none of the fresh and beguiling quality one might have expected from the title. The latest Music Hall offering is brightened occasionally by songs and dance routines. The plot is all about the familiar difficulties of putting on a Broadway show and it is the audition for this that brings on the few new personalities that the entertainment boasts. The best of them, to my mind, are Ann Miller, a rather good tap dancer, and the Three Chocolateers, who strut exuberantly. The songs (ten tunesmiths worked on these) are mildly infectious and several of them have been worked into novel production numbers by Sammy Lee."

Ann dancing on the RKO-Radio lot.

Ann is at the extreme left.
Harriet Hilliard is the bride.

Release date: September 3, 1937

CAST

Joe Penner	JOE PENNER
Barry Saunders	GENE RAYMOND
Parky	PARKYAKARKUS
Mitzi	HARRIET HILLIARD
Oliver	VICTOR MOORE
Pauline	HELEN BRODERICK
Dr. Molnac	Billy GILBERT
Betty	Ann MILLER
Hotel manager	Richard Lane
Beggs	Franklin Pangborn
Mrs. Penner	Margaret Dumont

Countess Martos	Ann Shoemaker
Susan	Jane Rhodes
Mr. Van Tuyl	George Irving
Mrs. Van Tuyl	Winifred Harris
Maître d'hotel	Charles Judels

CREDITS

Director: William A. Seiter *Producer:* Edward Kaufman *Scenarists:* Bert Kalmer, Harry Ruby, Viola Brothers Shore *From a story by:* Joseph Santley *Music and lyrics:* Herb Magidson, Allie Wrubel, George Jessel, Ben Oakland *Dance director:* Sammy Lee *Musical director:* Roy Webb *Vocal Arranger:* Charles Henderson *Director of photography:* J. Roy Hunt, A.S.C. *Special effects by:* Vernon L. Walker, A.S.C. *Art director:* Van Nest Polglase *Associate art director:* Al Herman *Gowns by:* Edward Stevenson *Set dressing by:* Darrell Silvera *Recorded by:* John E. Tribby *Edited by:* Jack Hively *Running time:* 77 minutes.

SONGS

"So You Won't Sing," "Let's Have Another Cigarette," "The Life of the Party," "Yankee Doodle Band," "Chirp a Little Ditty," "Roses in December."

SYNOPSIS

En route to Santa Barbara are a musical comedy group headed by Maestro Molnac (Billy Gilbert) and his manager Beggs (Franklin Pangborn); Mitzi (Harriet Hilliard) and Pauline (Helen Broderick), a singer and her agent; Oliver (Victor Moore) and his charge, society scion Barry Saunders (Gene Raymond). When Mitzi's slipper is caught between two of the railroad cars, Saunders falls for her while trying to loosen the slipper.

At the Casa Barbara, Parky (Parkyakarkus), the house detective, is hired to find the owner of the slipper who has since eluded Saunders. Oliver reminds the twenty-seven-year-old Saunders that he will lose his three-million-dollar inheritance if he marries before he reaches thirty.

Molnac is performing at the hotel. Mitzi and Pauline register there, hoping to get an audition for Mitzi. Complications arise when Mitzi's mother, Countess Martos (Ann Shoemaker), arrives with her wealthy friend Mrs. Penner (Margaret Dumont) and Mrs. Penner's son, Joe (Joe Penner). The doting mothers are trying to make a match between Mitzi and Penner.

Later Saunders finally sees Mitzi again and proposes marriage for a date three years hence. Oliver wires Saunders' mother to come at once.

When Mitzi's shoe wardrobe is stolen she thinks Saunders is responsible. She goes to his room in a negligee, scolds him, and leaves. Saunders, in a dressing gown, follows, but has to hide in another room when the Countess, Mrs. Penner, and her son arrive. Saunders overhears the Countess's wedding plans for her daughter. But Mitzi fibs and tells them she is already married. Saunders takes the cue and helps the pretense.

Pauline and Oliver arrange a wedding party. Maestro Molnac will be in charge of the entertainment. Even now, Pauline is still scheming to arrange an audition, and she bribes Parky and Penner to abduct the act's featured singer. Mitzi steps in and performs, to Molnac's enjoyment.

While the festivities are proceeding Saunders' mother arrives. She is delighted with the match and reveals that her son is really thirty years old and that his inheritance is secure. Now, to everyone's wonderment, Mitzi and Saunders announce their betrothal.

CRITICAL REACTION

Variety:

"A mild musical which should prove fairish entertainment. There is no walloping name in the cast, but a stalwart lineup of featured players which will, in the aggregate, attract some biz. Tapstress Ann Miller does some solo stomping during the 'Doodle Band' number, but she's been allowed to follow the Eleanor Powell style too chosely. Even her military raiment for the number is a too close approximation of togs Miss Powell wore during the finale of *Broadway Melody of 1937*. Production doesn't look expensive but is thoroughly adequate. Direction O.K. and camera very good."

Marguerite Tazelaar in the
New York Herald Tribune:

"If the title of the new picture at the Rivoli and the billing of Joe Penner as star do not discourage you, the following words probably will not keep you from the theater either. Some of the tunes are bright, Miss Hilliard's singing is agreeable and the colossal champagne party at the end is impressive. It all depends how much of an addict you are of the life of the party to gauge your enjoyment of the wise cracks, gags, comics and scrambled story at the Rivoli."

"The Doodle Band"

With Jane Rhodes, Franklin Pangborn, and Billy Gilbert.

STAGE DOOR

Release date: September 18, 1937

CAST

Terry Randall (Sims)	KATHARINE HEPBURN
Joan Maitland	GINGER ROGERS
Anthony Powell	ADOLPHE MENJOU
Linda Shaw	Gail PATRICK
Catherine Luther	Constance COLLIER
Kaye Hamilton	Andrea LEEDS
Henry Sims	Samuel S. HINDS
Judy Canfield	Lucille BALL
Milbank	Jack Carson
Harcourt	Franklin Pangborn
Richard Carmichael	Pierre Watkin

Butch	Grady Sutton
Stage director	Frank Reicher
Bill	William Corson
Hattie	Phyllis Kennedy
Eve	Eve Arden
Annie	*Ann Miller*
Ann Braddock	Jane Rhodes
Mary	Margaret Early
Olga Brent	Norma Drury
Dizzy	Jean Rouverol
Mrs. Orcutt	Elizabeth Dunne
Dukenfield	Fred Santley
Madeline	Harriet Brandon
Susan	Peggy O'Donnell
Cast of play	Katharine Alexander, Ralph Forbes, Mary Forbes, Huntley Gordon
Aide	Lynton Brent
Elsworth, critic	Theodore Von Eltz
Playwright	Jack Rice
Chauffeur	Harry Strang
Baggageman	Bob Perry
Theater patron	Larry Steers
Actresses	Mary Bovard, Frances Gifford, Josephine Whittell, Ada Leonard, Mary Jane Shower, Diana Gibson, Linda Gray, Alison Craig, Lynn Gabriel
Pamela Blake	Adele Pearce
Eve's cat	Whitey the Cat
Script clerk	Jack Gardner
Waiter	Ben Hendricks, Jr.
Dancing instructors	Jack Gargan, Theodore Kosloff, Gerda Mora, Julie Kingdon
Taxi driver	Al Hill

And: Byron Stevens, D'Arcy Corrigan, Philip Morris

CREDITS

Director: Gregory La Cava *Associate producer:* Pandro S. Berman *Based on the play by:* Edna Ferber, George S. Kaufman *Screenplay:* Morrie Ryskind, Anthony Veiller *Art directors:* Van Nest Polglase, Carroll Clark *Interior decorator:* Darrell Silvera *Assistant director:* James Anderson *Makeup:* Mel Burns *Costumes:* Muriel King *Jewelry:* Trabert & Hoeffer, Inc., Maubonssin *Still photographer:* John Miekle *Musical score:* Roy Webb *Sound:* John L. Cass *Director of photography:* Robert De Grasse *Film editor:* William Hamilton *Running time:* 92 minutes.

SONG

Music and lyrics: Hal Borne, Mort Greene. "Put Your Heart into Your Feet and Dance."

SYNOPSIS

Socialite Terry Randall (Katharine Hepburn) arrives in New York to become an actress. She gets accommodations at the Footlights Club, a theatrical boarding house for aspiring actresses, and shares a room with Joan Maitland (Ginger Rogers). The two do not get along.

Food and men are the two main topics of conversation at the Club. Judy Canfield (Lu-

With Eve Arden, Lucille Ball,
and Ginger Rogers.

cille Ball) manages dinner invitations with
visiting Seattle lumbermen and gets Joan to
double date. Linda Shaw (Gail Patrick), whom
Joan also dislikes, is the current girl friend of
Anthony Powell (Adolph Menjou), a famous
theatrical producer.

It has been a year since Kay Hamilton
(Andrea Leeds) has had an acting job. To
save money, she goes without meals at the
Club. She has hopes of getting the leading role
in Powell's new production of *Enchanted April*.

Meanwhile Powell spots Joan and Annie
(Ann Miller) at an audition. He is taken with
Joan and arranges for the two dancers to get
a spot at the Club Grotto, a nightclub in
which he owns a half interest. When Powell
asks Joan out for a late supper, she accepts—
not only to spite Linda, but to insure the
dance job she and Annie have at Powell's
club. Joan becomes his new companion.

Kay's appointment for a reading of the
part in *Enchanted April* is cancelled and she
faints in Powell's outer office. Terry tells Powell
off for not being available to see prospective
actors.

Richard Carmichael (Pierre Watkin), acting on behalf of a client, Henry Sims (Samuel
S. Hinds), makes Powell an offer for Terry to
play the part in his new show. Later in Powell's
apartment, Terry tries to expose Powell to Joan
as a phony. But Joan believes she is there only
because the two roommates do not get along
with each other.

Kay is suffering from malnutrition. At her
birthday party Catherine Luther (Constance
Collier) tells her that Terry has been signed
for the part.

Rehearsals go badly, but Carmichael's
client, who is in reality Terry's father, will
not let Powell out of the agreement.

On opening night, Kay comes to see
Terry. She gives her advice on how to play a
particularly difficult scene. Kay is despondent
and later commits suicide by jumping out of
a window.

Joan tells Terry about Kay's death, feeling
Terry is responsible. Terry is distraught, but
Catherine, who has been coaching her, tells
her that she must perform. Terry is superb in
the play. In her curtain speech she mourns

Ann and Ginger dance "Put Your Heart into Your Feet and Dance."
In the foreground: Gail Patrick, Franklin Pangborn, Adolphe Menjou.

Kay. Joan is moved by the tribute and the two become friends.

As the hit show continues into its fourth month, the routine at the Footlights Club remains the same. A new hopeful actress arrives to begin residence at the club.

CRITICAL REACTION

Frank S. Nugent
in the *New York Times:*

"The RKO-Radio version of *Stage Door* is not merely a brilliant picture (although that should be enough) but happens to be a magnificently devastating reply on Hollywood's behalf to all the catty little remarks that George Kaufman and Edna Ferber had made about it in their play. Miss Hepburn and Miss Rogers seemed to be acting so far above their usual heads that, frankly, we hardly recognized them. A round of curtain calls would demand a bow and smile from Constance Collier, Lucille Ball, Franklin Pangborn, Eve Arden, Ann Miller, Margaret Early and Phyllis Kennedy, among the many others."

Variety:

"It isn't *Stage Door*, as written by Edna Ferber and George S. Kaufman, but that is not likely to bother the film public that never saw the play. It is funny in spots, emotionally effective occasionally, and generally brisk and entertaining. It will do business. [The screenplay] is a spotty job which has been smoothed over by some good acting by the three stars and several of the featured players."

Howard Barnes in the
New York Herald Tribune:

"The making of *Stage Door* into a film has been a matter of splendid transmutation. It has come to the screen as a true motion picture. Brilliantly written, directed and acted. To my mind it is a far more satisfying entertainment than was the Edna Ferber–George S. Kaufman play. The lesser scenes, describing the minor triumphs and defeats of the girls who would be actresses, are beautifully timed and alternated. *Stage Door* is a remarkable job of making over stage material into a genuine film outline. It is a brilliant, witty and moving show."

With Ginger Rogers and Lucille Ball.

With Ginger Rogers and Adolphe Menjou.

RADIO CITY REVELS

Release date: February 11, 1938

CAST

Lester Robin	BOB BURNS
Harry Miller	JACK OAKIE
Kenny Baker	KENNY BAKER
Billie Shaw	ANN MILLER
Paul Plummer	Victor MOORE
Teddy Jordan	Milton BERLE
Gertie Shaw	Helen BRODERICK
Jane Froman	Jane FROMAN
Squenchy	Buster WEST
Lisa	Melissa MASON
Crane	Richard Lane

Delia Robin . . . . Marilyn Vernon
Announcer . . . . Don Wilson
And: HAL KEMP and His Orchestra

CREDITS

Director: Ben Stoloff *Producer:* Edward Kaufman *Screenplay:* Eddie Davis, Matt Brooks, Anthony Veiller, Mortimer Offner *Original story by:* Matt Brooks *Musical director:* Victor Baravalle *Lyrics:* Herb Magidson *Music:* Allie Wrubel *Vocal arrangements by:* Harry Simeone *Musical production numbers directed by:* Joseph Santley *Dances staged by:* Hermes Pan *Photographed by:* J. Roy Hunt, A.S.C., Jack Mackenzie, A.S.C. *Special effects by:* Vernon L. Walker, A.S.C. *Art director:* Van Nest Polglase *Associate art director:* Al Herman *Gowns by:* Edward Stevenson *Recorded by RCA Victor System Set dressing by:* Darrell Silvera *Recorded by:* Earl A. Wolcott *Montage by:* Douglas Travers *Film editor:* Arthur Roberts *Running time:* 90 minutes.

SONGS

"I'm Takin' a Shine to You," "Take a Tip from the Tulip," "Swingin' in the Corn," "(There's a) New Moon Over the Old Mill," "Goodnight Angel," "Speak Your Heart."

SYNOPSIS

At Radio City's NBC studios, Kenny Baker (Kenny Baker) is singing with Hal Kemp's Orchestra when his song is disrupted by the tap dancing of Billie Shaw (Ann Miller). Billie is delivering a Harry Miller (Jack Oakie) song to radio producer Paul Plummer (Victor Moore).

Miller and his pianist Teddy Jordan (Milton Berle), give songwriting lessons by mail order. Miller's songs are terrible, but he's still trying to sell the score for *Radio City Revels*.

One of Miller's pupils, Lester Robin (Bob Burns) of Van Buren, Arkansas, is discouraged. It seems that he can dream beautiful melodies but can't remember them once

he awakens. His sister Delia suggests that he go to New York to take his last four lessons in person.

When he arrives at Miller's apartment, Robin falls for Billie, and Billie's sister Gertie (Helen Broderick) falls for Robin.

Plummer needs a new theme song for his radio show. When Miller and Jordan accidentally discover Robin's "sleep writing," they copy his tune and it becomes a big hit.

Baker proposes to Billie. When Robin asks Gertie's advice on how to propose, Gertie believes the proposal is for her. She also discovers Miller's fraud when Robin falls asleep on her shoulder and begins "sleep writing."

Miller has now secured the contract to write the score for *Radio City Revels* but needs to come up with one more song by noon of the next day. When Robin finds out that Billie is engaged to Baker, he can't go to sleep. Miller and Jordan frantically try everything to make Robin sleepy. Later, Billie telephones Robin her good news about being in the show and says marriage can wait. Relieved, Robin falls asleep and Miller gets his song.

During the show, as Gertie tries proving to Plummer that Miller has stolen the songs, Jordan accidentally lets the truth out. But Robin feels that Miller really gave him his chance. Miller graciously announces the finale song as written by his latest protégé, Lester Robin. Billie gets her contract and Gertie gets Robin.

CRITICAL REACTION

Variety:

"*Radio City Revels* is a slight disappointment, partly because of the cast which, on paper, would suggest something much better. Kenny Baker, while singing his numbers well, is otherwise a screen disappointer, especially in romantic scenes. Most definitely on the way in is Ann Miller who has done minor tap-

With Kenny Baker.

dancing roles in a few pictures before getting this chance. She carries the romantic interest well, is a cute charming personality and has a lot of poise which Baker seems to lack opposite her. Miss Miller is a right smart tapster on the Eleanor Powell order."

Bosley Crowther in the
New York Times:

"With Jack Oakie and Milton Berle as a couple of dried-up songwriters, and with Bob Burns as an aspiring tunesmith from the sticks who unwittingly sings new songs in his sleep . . . [*Radio City Revels*] definitely has something to start with. It is only too bad that the songs which Bob dreams are not as inspired as his drollery. Aside from the above-mentioned zanies (and, grudgingly, Berle is included), the picture does count upon its credit side two such experts in their vein as Helen Broderick and Victor Moore, a nimble and beauteous little dancer named Ann Miller, and Buster West in a lively dance routine. But Kenny Baker is a total loss, there is no intelligent or artful presentation of the songs and—for that matter, as mentioned—there are really no songs worth presenting. Somehow a musical picture is always better off for a few."

R. W. D. in the
New York Herald Tribune:

"*Radio City Revels* is like a four-ring circus with occasional musical interludes for stomach relaxation. Current stars of the radio throw all their talents into one heap; the director, Ben Stoloff, gives it a touch worthy of George Abbott, and the result is a musical comedy that may set a trend for this type of screen medium. In spite of several likeable tunes, sung well by Kenny Baker and Jane Froman; in spite of two or three stunning production numbers, of an unobtrusive romance between Baker and Ann Miller, this film is more of a comedy than a musical comedy. A little more of Hal Kemp's music might have been in order, but the producers are to be congratulated for using the soft pedal on production numbers."

With Milton Berle and Jack Oakie.

With Milton Berle, Jack Oakie, and Helen Broderick.

Radio City Revels finale.

Release date: July 1, 1938

CAST

Teddy Shaw	GINGER ROGERS
Chick Kirkland	DOUGLAS FAIRBANKS, JR.
Fay Coleman	Peggy CONKLIN
Miriam	Lucille BALL
Buzzy Armbruster	Lee BOWMAN
Itchy Faulkner	Richard (Red) SKELTON
Vivian	Ann MILLER
P. U. Rogers	Donald MEEK
Henrietta	Eve Arden
Maxine	Dorothea Kent
Emil Beatty	Jack Carson

Mr. G	Clarence H. Wilson
Mac	Allan (Rocky) Lane
Gus	Grady Sutton
Shrimpo	Shimen Ruskin
Frances	Dorothy Tree
Mrs. Shaw	Leona Roberts
Mr. Shaw	Harlan Briggs
Emma	Inez Courtney
Mabel	Juanita Quigley
Henry	Kirk Windsor
Charlie	Dean Jagger
Subway riders	Hooper Atchley, Ronnie Rondell
Fresh subway rider	George Meeker
Singer	Betty Rhodes
Office supervisor	Elsie Cavanna

With

Mary Bovard, Frances Gifford, Peggy Montgomery, Baby Marie Osborne, Mary Jane Irving, Wesley Barry, Dorothy Moore, Stanley Brown, Etienne Girardot, Margaret Seddon, Kay Sutton, Dorothy Day, Lynn Bailey, Tommy Watkins, Cynthia Hobard Fellows, Steve Putnam, Bill Corson, Bob Thatcher, Ben Carter, Russell Gleason, Florence Lake, Vera Gordon, Margaret McWade.

CREDITS

Director: Alfred Santell *Producer:* Pandro S. Berman *Based on the play by:* Arthur Kober *Screenplay:* Arthur Kober *Musical director:* Roy Webb *Director of photography:* Robert de Grasse *Art directors:* Van Nest Polglase, Perry Ferguson *Set decorator:* Darrell Silvera *Sound recorder:* John E. Tribby *Dialogue director:* Ernest Pagano *Miss Roger's gowns by:* Renie *Wardrobe supervisor:* Edward Stevenson *Makeup:* Mel Burns *Special photographic effects:* Vernon L. Walker *Assistant director:* James Anderson *Still photographer:* John Miehle *Film editor:* William Hamilton *Running time:* 70 minutes.

SONGS

Music and lyrics: Charles Tobias, Sammy Stept, Bill Livingston. "Nighty Night," "My First Impression of You."

SYNOPSIS

Teddy Shaw (Ginger Rogers), a stenographer, goes to Kamp Kare-Free on a vacation. She leaves behind a nagging family and her ex-fiancé, Emil Beatty (Jack Carson).

At the resort she meets Chick Kirkland (Douglas Fairbanks, Jr.), a young law graduate. Kirkland is working as a waiter at the camp. Teddy shares quarters with her girl friends Fay Coleman (Peggy Conklin), Miriam (Lucille Ball), and Henrietta (Eve Arden). Fay tries in vain to interest Teddy in the camp's most eligible bachelor, Buzzy Armbruster (Lee Bowman). Teddy and Kirkland discover they are in love with each other, despite their frequent spats.

But, it all seems hopeless because Kirkland has no means of supporting a wife. He suggests that they should go ahead as if they were married. Teddy is shocked and angrily leaves him.

Later, in order to avoid Kirkland at a party, Teddy goes to Armbruster's bungalow where she falls asleep at a table. Armbruster doesn't disturb her. But when Teddy tries to sneak out of the bungalow the next morning Miriam sees her—and Miriam is jealous of Armbruster.

That morning Beatty arrives. In the dining room, Armbruster admits, mainly to annoy Miriam, that Teddy spent the night in his cabin. When Kirkland overhears this he punches Armbruster. Beatty berates Teddy for her indiscretion. He, too, is socked by Kirkland. Teddy and Kirkland are now back together and plan to marry in spite of Kirkland's financial prospects.

CRITICAL REACTION

Flin. in *Variety:*

"Much of the charm, romantic tenderness and social problem features of Arthur Kober's stage play, *Having Wonderful Time*, are missing in the screen version. With Ginger Rogers and Douglas Fairbanks, Jr., co-starred, neither adds to fame through this picture. It might have been an outstanding film with better adaptation and imaginative direction. Supporting players give good account of themselves . . . The joy, the awakening and the tragic tones of *Having Wonderful Time* are missing. The poetry of its love story is gone. It's just another film."

Frank S. Nugent in the *New York Times:*

"There was nothing genteel about Arthur Kober's *Having Wonderful Time* and—bless its folksy heart—there was nothing gentile either. But RKO-Radio's film version, which came into the Music Hall yesterday, is both. Mr. Kober's hillbillies from the Bronx are *alle goyim* now. The film leans a bit heavily on the romantic side—sometimes more heavily than the structure can bear. But generally the show is smooth, well-tempered, gently satiric."

R. W. D. in the *New York Herald Tribune:*

"The acting of capable Ginger Rogers helps to make this screen version more than a Bronx rhapsody in a country setting. *Having Wonderful Time*, in screen form, is an interesting cross-section of life, a little too pretty perhaps, but sufficiently heart-tapping to justify its existence as human entertainment for humans. *Having Wonderful Time* should amuse you."

It's cold on the set. Ann and friend bundle up.

Release date: September 28, 1938

CAST

Alice Sycamore	JEAN ARTHUR
Martin Vanderhof	LIONEL BARRYMORE
Tony Kirby	JAMES STEWART
Anthony P. Kirby	EDWARD ARNOLD
Kolenkhov	Mischa AUER
Essie Carmichael	*Ann MILLER*
Penny Sycamore	Spring BYINGTON
Paul Sycamore	Samuel S. HINDS
Poppins	Donald MEEK
Ramsey	H. B. WARNER
DePinna	Halliwell Hobbes

Ed Carmichael	Dub Taylor
Mrs. Anthony Kirby	Mary Forbes
Rheba	Lillian Yarbo
Donald	Eddie Anderson
John Blakely	Clarence Wilson
Professor	Josef Swickard
Maggie O'Neill	Ann Doran
Schmidt	Christian Rub
Mrs. Schmidt	Bodil Ann Rosing
Henderson	Charles Lane
Judge	Harry Davenport

BITS

Hughes Wallis Clark *Office manager* Paul Irving *Kirby's attorneys* Pierre Watkin, Edwin Maxwell, Russell Hicks, Eddie Kane *Douglas* Ien Wulf *Hammond* Chester Clute *G-men* Edgar Dearing, Ward Bond *Tart* Pert Kelton *Reporter* Gene Morgan *Attorney* Stanley Andrews *Mr. Leach* Walter Walker *Captain of waiters* Irving Bacon *Lord Melville* Robert Greig *Mary* Gladys Blake *G-men* James Burke, Eddy Chandler *Jailer* James Flavin *Brainy* Dick Curtis *Bank executives* Edwin Stanley, Edward Keane *Bank manager* Edward Earle *Attorney* Boyd Irwin *Expressman* Pat West *Mac* Frank Shannon *Captain Drake* John Hamilton *Mrs. Drake* Laura Treadwell *Mrs. Leach* Doris Rankin *Lady Melville* Hilda Plowright *Secretary* Byron Foulger *Matron* Blanche Payson *Reporters* Lou Davis, Lester Dorr, William Arnold, Jack Gardner *Police sergeant* James Farley *Neighbors* Eddie Fetherston, Bess Flowers, Beatrice Curtis, Beatrice Blinn, Bessie Wade, Eva McKenzie, Dorothy Vernon, Tina Marshall, Betty Farrington, Edward Peil, Sr., John Ince, Howard Davies, Charles Brinley, George Pearce, Eddie Randolph *Dopey* John Tyrrell *Court clerk* Edward Hearn *Bailiff* Lee Phelps *Policemen* James Millican, Bid Wiser, Jack Grant *Expressman* Vernon Dent *Dancers* Roland Dupree, Dorothy Babb, Joe Geil, Gloria Browne, Patty Thomas, Will Wolfstone *Blakely's secretary* Ann Cornwall *Bit men* Oliver Eckhardt, Homer Dickinson, Ralph McCullough *Bit women* Alice Keating, Nell Craig, Nell Roy *Secretary* Larry Wheat *Bobby* Eugene Anderson, Jr. *Guard* Charles Hamilton *Ice man* Dutch Hendrian *Bit man* Harry Semels *Trusty* Frank Mills *Bit man* Cy Schindell *Trusty* Sid D'Albrook *Guard* Charles MacMurphy *Bit men* Kit Guard, Robert Kortman, Lou King *Barber* Nick Copeland *Drunk* Clarence L. Sherwood *Bit man* Ernie Shields *Russian general in jail* Alex Woloshin *Women* Florence Dudley, Kitty Lanahan, Pearl Varvell, Gertrude Weber, Kay Deslys, Jane Talent, Georgia O'Dell *Bank guard* Dick Rush *Doorman* Harry Hollingsworth *Bank porter* Jimmy Adamson *Bank clerks* Dick French, Carlton Griffin, Carlie Taylor, Bruce Sidney *Elevator boy* Arthur Murray *Bank clerk* Harry Stafford *Neighbors* Frank Austin, Harry Bailey, Fred Parker, Bert Starkey, Frankie Raymond, Stella LeSaint, Belle Johnstone, Joe Bernard, Gale Ronn, Margaret Mann *Reporters* Bill Dill, William Lally *Taxi driver* Joe Bordeaux *Colored man* Jessie Graves *Bit men* Clive Morgan, Colonel Starrett Ford, Victor Travers, Wedgewood Nowell *Bit women* Rosemary Theby, Dagmar Oakland, Almeda Fowler, Hilda Rhodes *Accordion player* Mario Rotolo *Cop* Bruce Mitchell

CREDITS

Director and producer: Frank Capra *Based on the Pulitzer Prize play by:* George S. Kaufman, Moss Hart *Screenplay:* Robert Riskin *Assistant director:* Arthur Black *Director of photography:* Joseph Walker, A.S.C. *Art directors:* Stephen Gooson, Lionel Banks *Miss Arthur's*

gowns by: Bernard Newman, Irene *Musical director*: Morris Stoloff *Special score by*: Dimitri Tiomkin *Sound engineer*: Ed Bernds *Film editor*: Gene Havlick *Running time*: 127 minutes.

SYNOPSIS

Martin Vanderhof (Lionel Barrymore) made a decision thirty years before that he had enough money, and promptly retired. His family is eccentric, but they have fun. Penny Sycamore (Spring Byington), his daughter, writes plays and paints; her husband Paul (Samuel S. Hinds) manufactures fireworks; one of their daughters, Essie Carmichael (Ann Miller), makes candy and sells it. She also studies ballet with a Russian ex-wrestler, Kolenkhov (Mischa Auer).

The only sane member of the family is Alice (Jean Arthur). She is a secretary and is in love with her boss, Tony Kirby (James Stewart). Kirby, in turn, loves both Alice and her strange family.

Kirby brings his mother and father unexpectedly to dinner at the Vanderhof residence. Anthony P. Kirby (Edward Arnold), a business tycoon, and Mrs. Kirby (Mary Forbes) find a characteristic three-ring circus in progress.

While the socially prominent Kirbys are there, the police raid the Vanderhof home. Everyone, including the Kirbys, is taken to jail on suspicion of anarchism. Soon after, Alice and Kirby break off their relationship.

But later, Kirby Sr. tries to recapture his youth by wrestling with Kolenkhov and challenges Vanderhof to a harmonica duel. A victory is scored for the Vanderhof way of life. Alice and Kirby are then reunited.

CRITICAL REACTION

Frank S. Nugent
in the *New York Times*:

"Pulitzer Prize plays do not grow on bushes, a circumstance which is bound to complicate their grafting to the cinema. *You Can't Take It with You* was a tremendously amusing play. Columbia's film of the play, which moved into the Music Hall yesterday, has had to jus-

With Edward Arnold,
Mischa Auer, and Mary Forbes.

Ann has landed on Dub Taylor;
helping are Halliwell Hobbs,
Samuel Hinds, and Spring Byington.

tify the Pulitzer award. Frank Capra, its director, and Robert Riskin, its adapter, have vindicated that Pulitzer award, even at the expense of comedy. The characters Messrs. Kaufman and Hart invented were not undimensional after all. Vanderhofs, Sycamores, and Kirbys all have substance now. Beyond doubt, none of them is quite so funny—except possibly the hungry Russian, the lit'ry Mrs. Sycamore, the ballet-dancing Essie—but they are far more likeable, far more human. It's a grand picture, which will disappoint only the most superficial admirers of the play. Columbia, besides contributing the services of its famous writing-directing team, has chosen its cast with miraculous wisdom. *You Can't Take It with You* jumps smack into the list of the year's best."

Char. in *Variety*:

"A strong hit on Broadway, *You Can't Take It with You* is also a big hit on film. This is one of the higher-priced plays to be bought by pictures in history, Columbia having taken the rights for $200,000. Production brought the negative cost to around a reported $1,200,000. It will get all of that back and much more. The comedy is wholly American, wholesome, homespun, appealing, and touching in turn. Stoutest comedy scenes revolve around the

action in the Vanderhoff home as everyone proceeds with what they want to do. Lionel Barrymore plays the harmonica, his married, middle-aged daughter is typing plays that'll never sell, with a kitten cutely used as a paperweight; one of her daughters is practicing dancing; her husband is at the xylophone, and others are testing firecrackers or doing something else. Capra moves these scenes into swing beautifully under smart timing. Miss Arthur acquits herself creditably. Stewart does satisfactorily in the love scenes. Others are tops from Lionel Barrymore down . . . Spring Byington, Ann Miller, Samuel S. Hinds, Donald Meek, Halliwell Hobbes, Dub Taylor and the visiting Mischa Auer plus Lillian Yarbo and Eddie Anderson."

Howard Barnes in the *New York Herald Tribune*:

"Wisdom and artistry have gone into the screen production of *You Can't Take It with You* to make an eminently satisfying entertainment. It was a challenging task which the brilliant director-writer team of Frank Capra and Robert Riskin had in transferring the Pulitzer prize-winning drama to the cinema. They have accomplished it triumphantly. The players are well chosen and at the top of their form. The performances are assured and balanced."

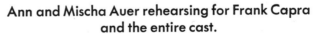

Ann and Mischa Auer rehearsing for Frank Capra and the entire cast.

ROOM SERVICE

Release date: September 30, 1938

CAST

Gordon Miller	GROUCHO MARX
Faker Englund	HARPO MARX
Harry Binelli	CHICO MARX
Christine	Lucille BALL
Hilda Manney	Ann MILLER
Leo Davis	Frank ALBERTSON
Gregory Wagner	Donald MacBride
Joseph Gribble	Cliff Dunstan
Timothy Hogarth	Philip Loeb
Sasha	Alexander Asro
Dr. Glass	Charles Halton
Simon Jenkins	Philip Wood

CREDITS

Director: William A. Seiter *Producer:* Pandro S. Berman *Based on the play by:* John Murray, Allen Boretz *Screenplay:* Morrie Ryskind *Art directors:* Van Nest Polglase, Al Herman *Set decorator:* Darrell Silvera *Musical director:* Roy Webb *Director of photography:* J. Roy Hunt *Assistant directors:* Philip Loeb, James Anderson *Film editor:* George Crone *Running time:* 78 minutes.

SONG

"Swing Low, Sweet Chariot."

SYNOPSIS

Room 920 in the White Way Hotel has been taken over by theatrical producer Gordon Miller (Groucho Marx), his associate Harry Binelli (Chico Marx), and his cast of twenty-two, while awaiting backing for a new show, *Hail and Farewell*. Payment of the hotel bill is overdue. Hotel executive Gregory Wagner (Donald MacBride), hoping to be promoted, tells Joseph Gribble (Cliff Dunstan), the hotel manager, to get rid of the troupe. Wagner wants to get the hotel into the black.

Christine (Lucille Ball), Miller's secretary, has lined up a potential backer to meet with him the next morning. Miller connives to stay in the suite until then. Leo Davis (Frank Albertson), the play's author, arrives unexpectedly and nearly broke. He is also put up in Room 920. It's love at first sight when Davis meets Hilda Manney (Ann Miller), a secretary, who has come to see the producer to line up an audition for her friend Sasha (Alexander Asro), a Russian waiter.

The next morning, Simon Jenkins (Philip Wood) arrives to tell Miller that a very wealthy man is ready to put fifteen thousand dollars in the play and will sign a check the following day. Davis pretends to have measles so the troupe cannot be evicted. But Davis wants to see Hilda and goes down to the hotel lobby. When Wagner and Gribble arrive, Faker Englund (Harpo Marx) pretends to be the sick man, with Christine in attendance as a nurse.

Dr. Glass (Charles Halton) discovers that Englund is not sick. The doctor is tied up and put in the bathroom.

Jenkins arrives to sign the check. But, when he fears publicity for his wealthy client, Fiske, he wants to renege on the deal. Upon being released, Dr. Glass, who has overheard everything, tells Wagner not to blow Miller's deal for the backing. Jenkins then signs the check and Miller gives it to Wagner to cover the troupe's hotel bills.

Davis then discovers that Jenkins signed the check only to get out of the madness of Room 920 and really intends to stop payment. Miller knows he has five days' credit until the transaction takes place through Fiske's California bank, and he decides to open *Hail and Farewell* in the hotel theater immediately.

When a bank clerk questions Wagner about a signature on a receipt of Miller's, Wagner finds out about Jenkins' stop payment order.

The play opens downstairs, but Wagner and the hotel detectives detain the four culprits in an upstairs suite. Davis fakes a suicide in order to try to get out of the suite to see his play. When Hilda sees that Davis is really alive she goes to keep an eye on the show.

Davis "dies." Wagner wants to get the body out of the hotel to avoid any scandal. At this point, to distract Wagner, Englund pretends that he has been stabbed and Englund is taken down to the back alley.

Meanwhile Davis is in the theater with Hilda, enjoying his success. Wagner faints when he sees Davis alive and when Englund is brought on stage at the finale of the play as a dead man. *Hail and Farewell* is a big hit.

CRITICAL REACTION

Variety:

"*Room Service* with the Marx Bros. is a natural for the boxoffice. Will do plenty of business and satisfy on the laugh score. The change of pace is a good idea and, basically, the Marxes have a more staple story structure upon which to hang their buffoonery. The

With Frank Albertson.

minimization of the musical highlights by the mute and Italian Marx brothers naturally points up Groucho's comedy all the more. Frank Albertson is the trusting young playwright from Oswego; Lucille Ball and Ann Miller are virtually walk-throughs as the femme vis-à-vis to Groucho and Albertson. As an entertainment, *Room Service* should maintain a very nice parity."

Frank S. Nugent in the *New York Times*:
"Just by way of gilding the lily, or painting a red nose on it, RKO-Radio has turned loose the mad Marxes upon the helter-skelter comedy known to Broadway last season and to the Rivoli yesterday as *Room Service*. To phrase it moderately, the Marxes haven't made it any funnier; but neither has their presence interfered to any large extent with the disorderly progress of an antic piece. While there may be some question about the play's being a perfect Marx vehicle, there can be none about it being a thoroughly daffy show. The film version is surprisingly close to the play.

Withal, *Room Service* remains a skylark and a comedy to be laughed at moderately if you saw the play, immoderately if you missed it."

**Howard Barnes in the
New York Herald Tribune:**
"The Marx Brothers have taken over a lusty stage hit for a clowning vehicle in *Room Service*. While the result is a generally entertaining burlesque, it is not nearly as hilarious as one might have anticipated. *Room Service* has passages of bright, comic business, but I don't think either the stars or the play have benefitted from the screen translation. The supporting company is fine, including such members of the original cast as Donald MacBride, in the part of the harassed hotel executive, and Alexander Asro as the waiter with a consuming desire to act. Lucille Ball and Ann Miller do what they can with the negligible feminine roles and Frank Albertson is excellent as the playwright. In his staging Mr. Seiter has kept the action moving and has accented the funniest portions of the film."

With Frank Albertson and Groucho Marx.

Groucho Marx, Lucille Ball, Chico Marx, Ann, and Harpo Marx.

Release date: October 28, 1938

CAST

Carol Vinson/"Sister Connie"	SALLY EILERS
Paul Montgomery	Lee BOWMAN
Violet McMaster	*Ann MILLER*
Mrs. Stockton	Alma KRUGER
Eddie Fox	Paul GUILFOYLE
Detective Lieutenant Cramer	Jonathan Hale
Reverend Summers	Hamilton MacFadden
Dan Bennett	Jack Arnold
Checkers	Robert Gleckler
A cripple	Byron Foulger
Reginald Roland	Cecil Kellaway
Jane Thompson	Janet Dempsey

CREDITS

Director: Leslie Goodwins *Producer:* B. P. Fineman *Screenplay:* Jo Pagano *Story and adaptation:* Saul Elkins *Production executive:* Lee Marcus *Musical director:* Frank Tours *Photographed by:* Nicholas Musuraca, A.S.C. *Art direction by:* Van Nest Polglase *Associate:* Albert D'Agostino *Gowns by:* Reale *Recorded by:* Hugh McDowell, Jr. *Edited by:* Desmond Marquette *Running time:* 68 minutes.

SONG

Music: Lew Brown; *lyrics:* Sammy Fain. "It's the Doctor's Orders."

SYNOPSIS

Young socialite Paul Montgomery (Lee Bowman) learns that his rich father has bought off his fiancée, Carol Vinson (Sally Eilers).

When the nightclub where Carol works is raided, the owner, Checkers (Robert Gleckler), with Carol's help, manages to escape. Detective Lieutenant Cramer (Jonathan Hale) is after racketeer Dan Bennett (Jack Arnold), who has sold stolen jewelry to the nightclub owner.

Carol and her pal Violet McMaster (Ann Miller) along with Vi's boyfriend, Eddie Fox (Paul Guilfoyle) form a vaudeville act, but Cramer follows and wrecks their plans.

The trio is nearly broke. When, at a revival meeting, Carol sees the size of the collection she decides to put on a revival show of her own. Evading Cramer, "Sister Connie," "Sister Violet," and "Brother Edward" are successful. The act is aided by fake "cures" in which cripples walk and the gullible audiences part with their money for Carol's collections.

Hearing rumors that "Sister Connie" is really Carol Vinson, both Montgomery and Cramer set out to find her. Later, when Carol spots Cramer in the audience, she tells the congregation she is a reformed sinner and, spoiling Cramer's game, announces that all contributions will go to the Children's Hospital.

Carol again refuses Montgomery's proposal. Instead she joins Bennett in a plot to steal a valuable necklace from Mrs. Stockton (Alma Kruger), who runs the hospital. Montgomery won't be dismissed and stays on.

Fox and Bennett arrange for a notorious fake cripple, Twisty Joe, to attend Carol's last night of revival, but he fails to show up. When Carol sees a cripple in the audience, she thinks he is the fake and goes into her act. The cripple walks. Carol is stunned when she learns the truth. Bennett refuses to give up the theft.

At Mrs. Stockton's, Jane Thompson (Janet Dempsey), a crippled girl, and her mother arrive, begging Carol to cure the girl. Carol, concerned, tries and fails. In agony, she confesses everything to the guests. Bennett tries to kill Carol for squealing but Cramer arrives in the nick of time and captures Bennett. Carol is forgiven and turns to Montgomery for comfort and a new life.

CRITICAL REACTION

Dorothy Masters in the *New York Daily News:*

"All attempts to polish up *Tarnished Angel* proved woefully porous in plot and characterization. Partly because RKO-Radio didn't loosen the purse strings and partly because they couldn't quite make up their minds on whether the screen play was a thriller, a comedy or a drama, this new film forfeits its birthright. If it's in Sally Eilers to be a great dramatic star, director Leslie Goodwins has neglected to give her his cooperation. While the plaudits for *Tarnished Angel* are pretty scarce, we might rake up a few for Jonathan Hale, Ann Miller, Paul Guilfoyle and Lee Bowman." (Two stars **)

Thomas M. Pryor in the *New York Times:*

"Our old friend the jewel thief is back again in *Tarnished Angel*. The trouble in this case seems to have originated in the script department and it apparently was communicated to the director who, in turn, passed it on to a capable troupe of players including Sally Eilers, Paul Guilfoyle, Ann Miller, and Lee Bowman. Somehow, we can't shake off the feeling

With Paul Guilfoyle and Sally Eilers.

that we've seen the story before, but under a different title, of course."

Wear. in Variety:

"*Tarnished Angel* turns out to be only weak, dual fare. Major difficulty is that there are abrupt voids in the action, unbelievable passages or uneven pace. Sally Eilers is competent though a little lightweight in revival meeting episodes as she travels cross-country with her former dancing chum and her boy friend. Lee Bowman is adequate in the few romantic scenes. Alma Kruger injects animation into the elderly rich village benefactor character. Paul Guilfoyle, as the male aid and pal of the two girls, is excellent, while Ann Miller, as the evangelist's girl chum, is passably fair. Cabaret episodes and police raid are well staged but contain virtually the sole excitement of the film."

R. W. D. in the
New York Herald Tribune:

"Sally Eilers tarnishes slowly, but not irrevocably in the RKO-Radio production film at the Rialto. There are moments when *Tarnished Angel* rises above its hereditary position—but these sequences are numbered and they are too disconnected to be very effective. With a cast that is a little too nice for the kind of roles called for, Leslie Goodwins has managed to impart in his direction an adequate co-ordination of ideas which keep the film on a straight track in spite of its unsatisfactory denouement. Miss Eilers gives a courageous performance. Lee Bowman has virtually nothing to do, Paul Guilfoyle is more a sourpuss than an evangelist's henchman and certainly no mate for pretty Ann Miller, and Jonathan Hale, a nice chap, has to play the goat as the persistent detective."

"It's the Doctor's Orders."

With Sally Eilers, Paul Guilfoyle, and Jonathan Hale.

Release date: November 8, 1940

CAST

Connie Casey	LUCILLE BALL
Clint Kelly	RICHARD CARLSON
Pepe	ANN MILLER
Jojo Jordan	EDDIE BRACKEN
Eileen Eilers	FRANCES LANGFORD
Al Terwilliger	HAL LE ROY
Manuelito	DESI ARNAZ
Tallulah Lou	Libby Bennett
Mr. Casey	Harry Shannon
Beverly Waverly	Douglas Walton
Lister	Chester Clute

Tiny person . . . . Midge Martin
Mrs. Tewksbury . . . . Ivy Scott
Sheriff Andaluz . . . . Byron Shores
Boy #41 . . . . Van Johnson
Boy . . . . John Benton
Co-eds . . . . Janet Lavis, Anna Mae Tessle,
Amarilla Morris, Vera Fern, Mildred Law, Ellen Johnson
Joe . . . . Michael Alvarez
Marie . . . . Sethma Williams
Detective . . . . Averell Harris
Hawker . . . . Tommy Graham
Football coach . . . . Grady Sutton
Butler . . . . Homer Dickinson
Indians . . . . Iron Eyes Cody, Jay Silverheels
Chief . . . . Chief John Big Tree
Student . . . . Pamela Blake

With Desi Arnaz and Hal LeRoy.

"Spic 'n' Spanish"

CREDITS

Director: George Abbott *Producers:* Harry Edington, George Abbott *Based on the play by:* George Marion Jr., Richard Rodgers, Lorenz Hart *Screenplay:* John Twist *Assistant director:* Dewey Starkey *Art director:* Van Nest Polglase *Dance director:* Le Roy Prinz *Special effects:* Vernon L. Walker *Director of photography:* Frank Redman *Film editor:* William Hamilton *Running time:* 84 minutes.

SONGS

Music and lyrics: Richard Rodgers, Lorenz Hart. "Heroes in the Fall," "You're Nearer," "Pottawatomie," "The Cakewalk," "Spic 'n' Spanish," "Love Never Went to College," "Look Out," "I Didn't Know What Time It Was," "The Conga."

SYNOPSIS

Clint Kelly (Richard Carlson) and Manuelito (Desi Arnaz), Princeton's two top football players, are working at The Hunted Stag, Kelly's aunt's lodge, while Manuelito decides where to go to college. Jojo Jordan (Eddie Bracken) of Harvard and Al Terwilliger (Hal Le Roy) of Yale arrive at the lodge to try to persuade Manuelito to go to their schools.

Mr. Casey (Harry Shannon), troubled by his daughter Connie (Lucille Ball), who has just arrived from Switzerland, offers Kelly a job as Connie's bodyguard with the promise of a job at Casey Allied Industries when he graduates. Connie tells her father that she is going to college at his alma mater, Pottawatomie, in Stop Gap, New Mexico. Girl crazy Manuelito decides Pottawatomie is the college for him, so Mr. Casey offers the four football players jobs as bodyguards.

On the way to New Mexico, Kelly sees Connie send a letter to writer Beverly Waverly (Douglas Walton), who lives near the college and is the real reason Connie has decided on Pottawatomie.

But the college is closed for non-payment of bills. Co-eds Pepe (Ann Miller) and Eileen Eilers (Frances Langford) tell the student body that they were unable to raise the needed three hundred dollars. The boys pool the money Mr. Casey has advanced them and the school is opened.

Kelly is falling for Connie, but the contract he signed with her father has an "anti-romantic" clause. Pottawatomie's football team needs help but Kelly, Jordan, and Terwilliger can't play. During a practice session Connie sees that Kelly really can play football. When Manuelito is hurt, his three friends go into the game. With the addition of these four top foot-

Pottawatomie victory dance.

ball players, Pottawatomie becomes the leading college team.

Connie is about to tell Kelly about her past when she gets a telegram informing her about the four bodyguards. She decides to leave that night for the East. The championship game is to be played the next day.

The townspeople are able to capture Manuelito, but the other three bodyguards are gone. On the day of the big game, Connie has a change of heart. Pottawatomie is behind. Waverly, who has found Kelly, Jordan, and Terwilliger, delivers them to the stadium. Connie apologizes. Love-struck Kelly goes into the game, and Pottawatomie is victorious.

CRITICAL REACTION

Kate Cameron in the
New York Daily News:
"Something to be thankful for this morning, if you are shopping for a good musical film, is that the George Abbott stage production of *Too Many Girls* has been transferred to the screen with its original score, some of its original cast and with the same zest and fast pace that distinguished it on Broadway. It's a lively picture with the same smart production background. The producers couldn't have selected a better Connie than Lucille Ball, who plays the wilful heiress of the story with zest. The ensemble numbers are nicely done, not too overwhelming, but a trifle more elaborate than the stage production. Richard Carlson, Ann Miller, Frances Langford and Libby Bennett help to make the picture thoroughly entertaining." (Three stars ***)

Walt. in *Variety:*
"George Abbott takes over the producer-director chores for the film version of his Broadway musical hit of last year. Outstanding factor of *Too Many Girls* to keep it from dipping into boredom, is its constant display of youthful effervescence and spontaneity. Despite lack of marquee values in the cast setup, there are some crackerjack performers in the lineup. Ann Miller, drafted from the George White

Scandals, does several fast solo dances, but in addition displays a fresh and youthful personality with plenty of showmanship behind it. This is Miss Miller's second try in Hollywood, after an unoptioned term at RKO about three years ago, and her performance and ability should tie her up as a permanent film fixture for filmusicals in the upper brackets. Picture is rich in production values and lavishness of the dance ensembles. LeRoy Prinz incorporates some new twists to the dances."

Bosley Crowther in the
New York Times:
"This has been an uncommonly indifferent football season on the screen, but RKO wound it up with a comfortable victory. The winning score was chalked by George Abbott's screen version of his Broadway musical success, *Too Many Girls.* It is mainly the young people—conceivable collegiates for a change—who give to *Too Many Girls* the snap and bounce that it has. Lucille Ball, Frances Langford, and Ann Miller are a trio of dangerous co-eds, and Richard Carlson and Eddie Bracken are a couple of smooth lads with the quips. At various moments, they all sing or dance with pleasing exuberance, and so do Desi Arnaz and Hal LeRoy."

Howard Barnes in the
New York Herald Tribune:
"There is a lot of fun in *Too Many Girls.* The songs have lost none of their lilting charm and the plot stands up well, for all of its fabulous collegiate antics. The feminine roles are played gaily and attractively on the screen by Lucille Ball, Frances Langford, and Ann Miller. Mr. Abbott has certainly kept the best aspects of his original production in making it into a picture. Those who didn't see the stage production of *Too Many Girls* will have a chance to see it now as a fairly entertaining screen musical."

Hal LeRoy, Ann, Richard Carlson, Lucille Ball,
Desi Arnaz, Frances Langford, Eddie Bracken.

Release date: October 15, 1940

CAST

David Farraday . . . . KENNY BAKER
Pat Abbott . . . . FRANCES LANGFORD
Ferdinand Farraday . . . . HUGH HERBERT
Emily Potter . . . . MARY BOLAND
Annabelle Potter . . . . ANN MILLER
Judy Abbott . . . . Patsy KELLY
Charles Moore . . . . Phil SILVERS
Soda clerk . . . . Sterling HOLLOWAY
Harrison . . . . Donald MacBRIDE
Mr. Pasley . . . . Barnett PARKER
Carter . . . . Franklin PANGBORN

Specialties

SIX HITS and A MISS,
BORRAH MINEVITCH
and HIS HARMONICA RASCALS.

CREDITS

Director: John H. Auer *Associate producer*: Sol C. Siegel *Original screenplay*: Bradford Ropes, F. Hugh Herbert, Maurice Leo *Additional comedy sequences*: Sid Kuller, Ray Golden *Musical director*: Cy Feuer *Orchestral arrangements*: Walter Scharf, Gene Rose *Dance director*: Danny Dare *Production manager*: Al Wilson *Director of photography*: Jack Marta *Supervising editor*: Murray Seldeen *Art director*: John Victor Mackay *Wardrobe*: Adele Palmer *RCA "High Fidelity" recording Film editor*: William Morgan *Running time*: 88 minutes.

SONGS

Music and lyrics: Jule Styne, Walter Bullock. "Who Am I," "In the Cool of the Evening," "Make Yourself at Home," "Swing Low, Sweet Rhythm," "The Swap Shop Song," "The Trading Post," "Sally," "Ramona," "Dinah," "Margie," "Sweet Sue," "Mary Lou."

SYNOPSIS

Station WPX's important accounts are switching to large network stations and Harrison (Donald MacBride), the station manager, doesn't know how to keep the station from going into bankruptcy. The Farraday Trading Post, a Connecticut suburb swap shop, is an important account of WPX. But David Farraday (Kenny Baker) tells his uncle Ferdinand (Hugh Hubert) that the radio program has to be discontinued as an economy move.

Harrison, accompanied by singers Pat Abbott (Frances Langford) and Judy Abbott (Patsy Kelly), goes to the Connecticut shop to try to persuade Farraday to stay with the station. Dotty Uncle Ferd swaps the shop for the insolvent broadcasting station.

Since television is beginning to emerge, Uncle Ferd borrows money for expensive television equipment for the station, using the Trading Post as security for the loan. Since he no longer owns the shop, the bank note must be met within the ninety-day period or he will face criminal prosecution.

Mrs. Emily Potter (Mary Boland), a wealthy Brooklyn department store owner, is impressed by David's management of WPX and decides to sponsor a program. Her only stipulation is that her daughter Annabelle

With Kenny Baker and Frances Langford.

"Pan America Conga"

(Ann Miller) be used as the show's singing star. Annabelle can dance, but singing is not her forte. Pat agrees to actually do the singing off-camera, without Annabelle's knowledge. Pat, in love with David, sacrifices her career and Annabelle is heralded as WPX's golden-voiced singing star.

In order to make publicity appearances with Annabelle, David frequently breaks dates with Pat. Judy is angry about David's thoughtlessness, but Pat refuses to expose the hoax. During a telecast, Judy switches the controls so that Annabelle's real voice is heard.

When the truth is known, Mrs. Potter reassures David and Uncle Ferd that she will continue her sponsorship. It seems her store is enjoying increased business as a result of the show. Pat is now featured as the singing star and Annabelle is pleased to be able to concentrate on her dancing.

CRITICAL REACTION

Kate Cameron in the
New York Daily News:

"Republic Pictures have failed to repeat the success they had in the original *Hit Parade* in the latest film of the same name. *Hit Parade of 1941* is a loosely-strung series of variety acts and ancient gags. Frances Langford, the only member of the cast who was in the 1937 version of *Parade*, introduces several new tunes and sings them with sweetness and charm. Kenny Baker plays opposite Miss Langford and assists her in putting over the new songs. His voice and Miss Langford's and a tap routine done expertly by the nimble-footed Ann Miller are the picture's chief assets." (Two stars **)

The *Hollywood Reporter*:

"Zestful, melodious musical numbers of the hit variety, capably presented, with Frances

Langford and Kenny Baker scoring heavily on the vocal side, superb dancing by Ann Miller, and the rib-tickling comedy of Hugh Herbert give *The Hit Parade of 1941* numerous high points of entertainment. As Republic's most ambitious venture into the filmusical field, it is a creditable effort, well-produced. Frances Langford and Kenny Baker provide the romantic interest, with Ann Miller taking time off between dances to portray the feather-brained menace to their happiness. There should be a law against Ann Miller's ever taking time off from dancing. The beauty, brilliance and consummate grace of her artistry is an endless delight. Her final number is the high point of the picture."

The Film Daily:

"Embracing much comedy, clever singing and dancing, the newest edition of the *Hit Parade* series has a great deal to offer in the way of entertainment. Director John H. Auer has effectively blended the various elements of the musical comedy. Easily one of the highlights of the picture is the dancing of beautiful Ann Miller. Cy Feuer rates credit for directing the music."

Thomas M. Pryor
in the *New York Times:*

"Republic has poured a lot of good-natured foolishness into the *Hit Parade of 1941*, but somehow the show falls flat, notwithstanding the presence of such expert zanies as Hugh Herbert, Mary Boland, Phil Silvers, and Patsy Kelly. Musically, the film fares somewhat better, for Frances Langford and Kenny Baker know how to put a song over. Plot sets Miss Langford and Mr. Baker to billing and cooing and drags in Ann Miller as interference. Miss Miller makes the most of her conventional assignment and manages to get in a few lively tap dances. *Hit Parade of 1941* is not unlike the *Big Broadcast* shows which Paramount used to sponsor, but it is done with considerably less pretentiousness. With that we have no quarrel, however, for simplicity of design is the film's chief asset."

"Swing Low, Sweet Rhythm"

MELODY RANCH

Release date: November 15, 1940

CAST

Gene . . . . GENE AUTRY
Cornelius J. Courtney . . . . JIMMY DURANTE
Julie Shelton . . . . ANN MILLER
Mark Wildhack . . . . Barton MacLAINE
Veronica Whipple . . . . Vera VAGUE
Pop . . . . George "Gabby" HAYES
Tommy Summerville . . . . Jerome COWAN
Penny . . . . Mary LEE
Jasper Wildhack . . . . Joseph Sawyer
Bud Wildhack . . . . Horace MacMahon
Judge Henderson . . . . Clarence Wilson
Slim . . . . William Benedict
and: CHAMPION

CREDITS

Director: Joseph Santley *Associate producer:* Sol C. Siegel *Screenplay:* Jack Moffitt, F. Hugh Herbert *Special comedy sequences:* Sid Kuller, Ray Golden *Production manager:* Al Wilson *Director of photography:* Joseph August *Supervising editor:* Murray Seldeen *Art director:* Joseph Victor Mackay *Musical director:* Raoul Kraushaar *Wardrobe:* Adele Palmer *Film editor:* Lester Orlebeck *Running time:* 84 minutes.

SONGS

Special music and lyrics: Jule Styne, Eddie Cherkose. "Melody Ranch," "Never Dream the Same Dream Twice," "Torpedo Joe," "What Are Cowboys Made Of?," "Rodeo Rose," "Call of the Canyon," "Back in the Saddle Again," "Vote for Autry," "Welcome Back Home," "Go Back to the City Again," "My Gal Sal."

SYNOPSIS

Popular radio entertainer Gene Autry returns to his home town, Torpedo, as the guest of honor of the Frontier Days Celebration. He is also honorary sheriff. Cornelius "Corney" J. Courtney (Jimmy Durante) insisted that Autry accept the invitation, for he believes the publicity will counterbalance Autry's damaged reputation since Julie Shelton (Ann Miller), a debutante with theatrical aspirations, has been on his program.

The Wildhack brothers, Mark (Barton MacLaine), Jasper (Joseph Sawyer), and Bud (Horace MacMahon), Autry's childhood enemies, are now the local gangsters. The brothers own a saloon next door to the school, and the safety of the children is endangered by the brawling. Autry plans to expose this situation during his next broadcast direct from Torpedo. The Wildhacks stop the broadcast and beat Autry up.

Hollywood has softened Autry, and he is

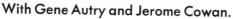

With Gene Autry and Jerome Cowan.

humiliated by not being able to defend himself from his assailants. He decides to remain in Torpedo and get into condition. Autry is encouraged by Corney, Pop (George "Gabby" Hayes), and his pert granddaughter Penny (Mary Lee). Pop runs the local trolley which carries Autry's fans to his show.

Julie now sees Autry in his natural setting and becomes interested in the cowboy whom she formerly scorned.

When Autry rounds up the Wildhacks, licking them single handedly, he forces them to sing on his radio broadcast. The brothers are enraged by this humiliation and vow to get Autry. Autry now decides to run for sheriff so that he will be able to clean up the Wildhack political machine and make Torpedo a respectable town once again.

In a battle, one of Autry's friends is killed. Autry finally secures the evidence which irrefutably labels the brothers as the killers. Julie confesses her love to Autry, and they become engaged.

CRITICAL REACTION

Wanda Hale in
the *New York Daily News:*
"*Melody Ranch*, Gene Autry's latest with Jimmy Durante, is unfortunate for both the popular singing cowboy and the loveable, hard-working comedian. They just weren't made to be in the same picture. Republic's fancying up of the old western formula results in an almost unbearably slow moving vehicle. Durante gives the picture an occasional shot in the arm but the effect wears off and the film relapses into listlessness when he disappears from the scene. Ann Miller is a decorative young lady and a fast stepping dancer but she has to go about registering 'love' so much that you'll have an urge to yell 'cut' to the cameraman." (Two stars **)

The Film Daily:
"*Melody Ranch*, the Gene Autry special with which Republic hopes to crash the few theaters which are not regular Autry customers,

"My Gal Sal"

1005-167

With Jimmy Durante.

is fun—swell fun. Its 84 minutes pass all too quickly and leave the audience with a taste for more of the knock-out comedy sketches, certainly much more of Ann Miller's inimitable dancing. Gene Autry was never better. . . . Jimmy Durante has one of the best roles ever given him in films and how he does go to town! Ann Miller is grand, lovely to look at, and her one dance number is rhythmic perfection. Joseph Santley's direction brings the clever comedy to lusty life and aids the principals materially. The Sol C. Siegel production is one of Republic's best."

A. H. Weiler in the *New York Times:*
"To the marble-and-jacks set another Gene Autry picture is an event as welcome as the Christmas holidays. For that reason, then, *Melody Ranch* which arrived at the Bryant yesterday, is another gaudy bauble to pluck from a laden tree. But Republic apparently intended the film for a wider audience, weighting this super-Western with romance, radio programs and comedy and the varied talents of such eminent non-Westerners as Jimmy Durante, Ann Miller, Jerome Cowan and Barton MacLaine. The result, however, falls short of expectations—for many reasons, the chief of which is the story, which even Autry fans

might consider a bit on the thin side. This time, for instance, Mr. Autry, as a radio singing star, returns to his racket-ridden home town as an honorary sheriff, dispatches the three responsible scalawags and, justice done, he finally wins the girl. It is an old vehicle and the going is tough."

E. G. in the *New York Herald Tribune:*
"Gene Autry, the singing cowboy of radio and screen, must feel more at ease astride a bucking broncho than he does in *Melody Ranch*, his latest cinematic endeavor at the Bryant Theater. In Republic Picture's latest horse opera—a medley of ancient corny jokes, juvenile plot and forced acting interspiced with an agreeable song or two—Mr. Autry surely does not personify an Eastern tenderfoot's conception of a hard riding cowhand. He has a pleasant singing voice and can put across his songs, but the less said of his thespian efforts the better. Jimmy Durante, Ann Miller, George Hayes and Barbara Allen, the Vera Vague of the air waves, are among the more prominent players assisting Mr. Autry in an earnest effort to inject their respective bits of humor into the proceedings, but they succeed only in prolonging the sorry spectable of a tiring Western story."

THE
COLUMBIA
YEARS

Moviegoers sought relief from battle news, ration stamps, civil defense, and blackouts during World War II. They found it in the escapism produced by Hollywood and shown on the screens of local movie palaces. Ann Miller's staccato tap dancing in her Columbia musicals during the war years helped ease the tensions of millions of American civilians and service personnel. These movies were made quickly and cheaply. Filming took about four weeks and usually cost between $400,000 and $600,000. Yet all were profit-making motion pictures for the studio.

In 1941 Ann signed a one-picture deal with Columbia. The picture was *Time Out for Rhythm*. Harry Cohn, the head of Columbia, was obviously pleased with Ann's reviews and her work in the picture. After its completion, she was promptly signed to a long-term contract.

Columbia may not have been, at that time, the most prestigious Hollywood studio, but at the Gower Street studios Ann was a *Star*. Cohn saved the Technicolor musicals for Rita Hayworth, so all of Ann's movies were filmed in black-and-white and ran scarcely over an hour-and-a-half. Ann's tapping and charisma made up for the budget restrictions and the absence of lavish production numbers.

In *Time Out for Rhythm* Ann had three dance routines, choreographed by LeRoy Prinz. Her big solo dance number was "A-Twiddlin' My Thumbs." Ann appeared as the maid to a nightclub singing star, played by Rosemary Lane. Rudy Vallee, Rosemary's agent, discovers Ann's dancing talent. This corny Cinderella story also featured Ann in a duet with Allen Jenkins, "Obviously the Gentleman Prefers to Dance."

Her third dance number was the title song finale, which *Variety* cited as being the best tune in the picture for popular appeal.

Glen Gray's Casa Loma Band highlighted the band's instruments in its one musical number in white against a black background, thus making the performing musicians appear invisible.

Since Ann's hands were just as expressive as her lightning feet, the studio insured them for twenty-five thousand dollars during the filming of her first Columbia contract feature film. This was a typical example of the kind of studio publicity stunts fabricated for the gullible movie audience who bought fan magazines.

Time Out for Rhythm was the kind of motion picture Ann referred to as a "nervous A"—not quite big enough to rate as a first-class motion picture, but having more production values than the movies designated for the second-feature slot on theater double bills.

Up-and-coming composer Saul Chaplin gave his special talents to the musical scores of Ann's Columbia films. Starting with *Time Out for Rhythm*, his name, as composer, arranger, etc., appears in the credits of Ann's films more than any other one person.

Chaplin began in the motion picture business in partnership with Sammy Cahn for Republic's *Rookies on Parade*. The team was then hired by Harry Cohn, just as Cohn was beginning to make a series of quickie musical films—*mostly* with Ann Miller. Sammy Cahn eventually teamed with Jule Styne, among others, but Chaplin stayed at Columbia. Chaplin has stated that he really learned the movie business at Columbia.

The talented composer has worked with the best and with the superstars. "For heaven's sake, don't leave out Ann Miller!" chortles Chaplin. "That's my real distinction! I have done more films with Ann Miller than anyone alive! The entire time I worked at Columbia, from 1940 to 1949, it was always Ann Miller. My life from 1940 to 1959 was Ann Miller, because when she moved to Metro, I did too! Believe me, I am the world's foremost authority on Ann Miller!" [1]

Go West, Young Lady, a musical western, paired Ann with lean, boyish Glenn Ford, and the star of Columbia's bread-and-butter *Blondie* series, Penny Singleton. Seeing Miss Singleton in a musical film was a treat. She had come from the Broadway musical-comedy stage and seemed to enjoy this change of pace from her *Blondie* stereotype. *Variety* remembered Miss Singleton from her legit stage appearances, when she was known as Dorothy McNulty. In its review for *Go West, Young Lady*, the show business paper wrote about her singing and dancing that "she gets one opportunity to do both in this picture, and cleans up solidly."

As Lola, a saloon entertainer, Ann danced on top of a bar. In this number, the title song of the picture, choreographer Louis DaPron backed up Ann with six chorus girls on the tiny saloon stage. After the vocal part of the number, Ann left the stage, was picked up and lifted to the bar, and danced the entire legnth of it. At the conclusion of the

1. Quoted in Max Wilk, *They're Playing Our Song* (New York: Atheneum, 1974), p. 206.

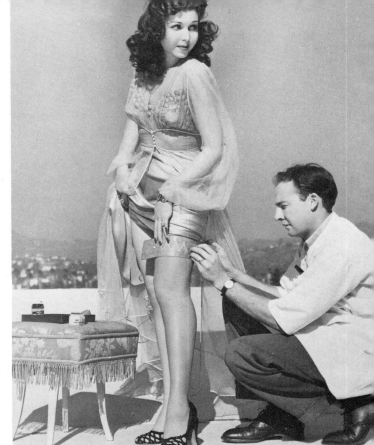

Leg guards were worn to protect Ann's shins from her spurs while recording taps for "I Wish That I Could Be a Singing Cowboy."

Leg makeup was used during the war instead of stockings. Here you see how it was done.

Ann does her bit to help the war effort.

Ann witnesses the check paid by Columbia studio executive William Behnke to Col. W. W. Hubs for the screen rights to *Hey, Rookie*.

number, back on the stage, Ann ended the routine in a split. The rowdy audience shot their guns into the air in approval.

Ann wore spurs in a comedy number tapping and rolling the spurs to music with Allen Jenkins. For two weeks Ann rehearsed "I Wish That I Could Be a Singing Cowboy," wearing special rubber leg guards to protect her legs while she was learning the routine. She and Miss Singleton also had a rowdy, free-for-all, hair-pulling fight which one reviewer said was worth the price of admission.

Starting with a two-picture loan-out to Paramount, Ann's next several movies usually had some sort of armed forces theme, with the army taking the most prominent place. *True to the Army* was basically a showcase for Judy Canova, whose films were then popular box-office attractions. Ann supplied the glamor, offsetting Miss Canova's hillbilly comedy. Tenor Allan Jones played opposite Ann, while Jerry Colonna was paired with Miss Canova for the laughs.

Ann set a new world record for tap-dance speed—an almost unbelievable speed of 840 taps to the minute—during rehearsals for *True to the Army*. The occasion was her "target range" tap routine, for which she was coached by the film's choreographer, Jack Donahue. The speed record's authenticity was attested to by Colonel Charles Ide, Army artillerist; Danny Dare, screen dance authority; and songwriter Johnny Mercer. Ann's routine was fimed on the stage of the Biltmore Theatre in Los Angeles. There was no audience except for the film crew. But in the previous year, Ann played the Biltmore with *George White's Scandals*. There was an audience then and she won her new movie contract at that time. "Jitterbug's Lullaby" and the picture's finale, "Wacky for Khaki," were Ann's other numbers.

Ann Miller as a blonde? Toplined in Paramount's *Priorities on Parade*, Ann allowed her jet-black hair to be bleached for the first and only time in her career. The experience was not a pleasant one. She remembers the process as disastrous; the damage done by the harsh bleach took a long time to repair. It is hard to imagine why anyone thought it a good idea to have two blonde leading ladies in the same film. Betty Rhodes, a minor star of Paramount's "B" musicals, was the other blonde.

Priorities on Parade was a salute to the women who worked in war plants. Ann, starting a career-role trend, leaves her co-workers to star in a nightclub show, but relents in time to rejoin her stalwart group for the finale. Ann celebrated her nineteenth birthday during the filming.

Jack Donahue also served as choreographer for this film. Donahue conceived a *sand dance*, a *radium dance*, and a *shadow dance*, along with a *black-out dance*, "Be Kind to Your Air Raid Warden," for Ann's dancing skills and for the comedy singing talent of Jerry Colonna. In the Eagle airplane factory, Ann danced to "I'd Love to Know You Better" and "Pay Day," a production number in the movie's revue finale entitled *Up In Arms*.

When New York's Paramount Theater showed *Priorities on Parade*, the stage show featured Ann Miller "in person" as an extra added attraction. Phil Harris and His Orchestra, Zero Mostel, and the Juvelys were also on the bill.

The true-life radio broadcasts of Jean Ruth, a wartime radio personality, served as the story outline for *Reveille with Beverly*, in which Ann played a radio disc jockey. When the "platters" were spun, movie audiences were treated visually to scenes of the top recording artists of the day. A very young, skinny singer named Frank Sinatra was part of the musical vignettes, singing "Night and Day," as were Lee and Lynn Wilde, who sang with the Bob Crosby orchestra. Later the Wilde Twins worked in many M-G-M musicals.

In every Ann Miller Columbia musical there was at least one show-stopping tap routine. *Reveille with Beverly* squeezed one in at the last minute, when Beverly made an "in person" appearance at an army post. The number was "Thumbs Up and V for Victory." It was worth the wait. Ann, cute as a button in an excellent tap routine, ended the number by dancing through a huge flaming "V." Ann wrote in her autobiography that this was the scene in which the flames from the "V" singed her costume, hair, and eyelashes. "One picture of mine," Ann remembers, "cost three hundred and fifty thousand dollars and made Columbia three million dollars!" That picture was *Reveille with Beverly*.

This World War II musical gave the boys overseas something to remember home by. A besieged garrison at Corregidor had only one film—*Reveille with Beverly*. To keep up morale, it was run over and over.

"I must have seen it at least a hundred times," General Douglas MacArthur personally told Ann when he met her in Hollywood. "You did quite a dance," the general said with a grin. "I'd know you anywhere."

With Walter Winchell.

Dancing partner Bill Shawn checks a pedometer on Ann's leg during *Hey, Rookie* rehearsals to clock her dance mileage.

A company of engineers in the South Pacific sent Ann this painting made of her during the filming of *Eve Knew Her Apples.*

In many movie houses during World War II, theater patrons could purchase war bonds in the lobby. The cost of a bond, $18.75, became the title of a popular song in *What's Buzzin' Cousin?* and the basis of a whirlwind tap number for Ann Miller. Eddie Anderson, widely known as Rochester on Jack Benny's radio show, sang a chorus of the song, and Ann's finish had her dancing right through a huge war-bond poster. The far-from-subtle patriotic suggestion probably sold quite a number of bonds during the intermission!

Publicity for *What's Buzzin' Cousin?* boasted that it had the largest number of songs in a Columbia musical. The picture's choreographer, Nick Castle, called Ann the best all-round female dancer of the past twenty years. This was quite an accolade, for Castle's list included Eleanor Powell, Vera Zorina, Adele Astaire, Marilyn Miller, and Marie Bryant.

Ann wanted to do a "Barefoot Stomp" in the picture, but the idea was scrapped because it was impossible to record barefoot taps. Leg makeup was worn for the first time in this movie by the chorus girls. Makeup artist Clay Campbell was responsible for concocting the liquid hose. (Silk had other war uses, such as being the primary material used in making parachutes. Nylon had yet to come into wide use.) Ann was responsible for the invention of pantyhose. The studio's wardrobe people would sew stockings onto her panties while Ann stood between scenes. It was a long and tiring process, so Ann called Willy de Mond who then made them all in one piece. Ann's other dance number in this motion picture was "Knocked Out Nocturne," in which she danced with the Freddy Martin band.

The money paid for the screen rights to *Hey, Rookie*, based on an original army show that had a Los Angeles run of thirty-six weeks, was donated to the Fort MacArthur recreation fund. The stage show had been done by the Yard Bird Club of Fort MacArthur. Ann acted as mascot for their football team during the filming of *Hey, Rookie*.

"Streamlined Sheik" served as Ann's big tap number, and it remains Ann's favorite dance number with drums from her Columbia years. Ann usually danced alone, or in front of a chorus. But in *Hey, Rookie* dance director Val Raset decided that, for the first time, Ann would dance with a partner; she and Bill Shawn (the former partner of Mayris Chaney, the well-known dancer who was sponsored by Eleanor Roosevelt) danced a lovely adagio to "Take a Chance." A set statistician attached a pedometer to Ann's leg during her dance rehearsals and clocked forty-eight miles of dancing during the twelve-day rehearsal period for the movie.

Hey, Rookie also showcased Joe Besser's fey comedy routines ("Oww, that hurts!") and featured specialties by the tap-dancing Condos brothers, a stand-up comedy monologue by Jack Gilford, and even a "B" Betty Hutton—the energetic Judy Clark who performed with the Solid Senders. A pre-*Jolson Story* Larry Parks played the love interest and even sang a couple of numbers without soundtrack help from Jolie.

Jam Session was merely an excuse for Columbia to cash in on the popular big-name bands of the era. The thin story line had Ann as a dance contest winner who goes to Hollywood and finally gets into the movies. But with six of the nation's most popular dance bands such as those of Charlie Barnet, Louis Armstrong, Alvino Rey, Jan Garber, Glen Gray, and Teddy Powell and vocalists like Nan Wynn and the Pied Pipers, the fans got exactly what was advertised, with one of Ann's specialty tap routines thrown in for the movie's finale.

"Victory Polka" was the flash finish. Bill Shawn again partnered Ann at the finish of the number.

Jam Session was the last of four Columbia musicals to be directed by Ann's favorite director on the lot, Charles Barton, who had previously directed her in *Hey, Rookie, Reveille with Beverly*, and *What's Buzzin' Cousin?* "He was very good," said Ann, "and those pictures made a mint!"

Ann's trademark—the abbreviated black sequin corset costume with long black stockings—was shown off in *Carolina Blues*.

Dancer Harold Nicholas, half of the famous Nicholas Brothers dance team, soloed in "Mr. Beebe." His brother, Fayard, was just being discharged from the service at this time. The long production number used one hundred chorus dancers. Ann sang the first chorus of "Mr. Beebe" but didn't dance in the number.

Kay Kyser dominated most of the screen time in this movie, and Ann had only one dance number, "Thanks a Lot," choreographed by Sammy Lee. The *Hollywood Reporter* wondered why Ann was allowed only this one dance routine. Surely her fans, upon seeing the movie, wondered the same thing. But Kyser wanted to spotlight his future wife, Georgia Carroll—a model who sang.

But Kyser's band was popular, and Columbia used his real-life war-bond tours as the basis for the plot of *Carolina Blues*. Official records show that Kyser actually sold over ninety million dollars in bonds. (*Battleship Blues* was the working title of the film.)

In 1944, choreographer Jack Cole started a dance workshop at Columbia. His group, which included Rod Alexander, and George and Ethel Martin, backed up Rita Hayworth in her musicals. Now Cole gave Ann's dance numbers style in *Eadie Was a Lady*.

Ann tapped to "I'm Gonna See My Baby." Cole and his dancers did the imaginative jazz routines for which the choreographer later became famous in his work with Betty Grable and Marilyn Monroe in their Twentieth Century-Fox musicals. In the title number, Ann even pulled up her period skirt for some quick tap steps. A Greek ballet in *Eadie Was a Lady* featured Ann tap dancing, jazz dancing by the chorus boys, while the toga-clad chorus girls danced with cymbals on their knees! It took Cole's genius to mold these diverse elements together for the movie's finale.

Because Ann was known primarily as a dancer, many people didn't realize just how good a singer she was. In all these Columbia musicals Ann sang—usually a ballad with little or no dancing. "You Came Along, Baby" was her song in *Eadie Was a Lady*. She had an excellent singing quality, sensuous and low-pitched, and she knew, with little formal vocal training, how to handle the lyrics of a song. (Interestingly enough, it wasn't until Ann appeared in *Mame* and *Sugar Babies* and on "The Merv Griffin Show" that anyone really knew that she ever sang.)

Her next film was quite a departure. *Eve Knew Her Apples* was a "B" remake of Columbia's Academy Award-winning film *It Happened One Night*, the zany comedy classic which starred Clark Gable, on loan to Columbia from M-G-M, and Claudette Colbert. A huge fight ensued at Columbia, and the result was that Harry Cohn and Irving Briskin were almost fired by remaking *It Happened One Night* with the innocuous title of *Eve Knew Her Apples*. The movie was Ann's first straight dramatic role at Columbia, with Ann playing the Claudette Colbert role. William Wright was cast in Clark Gable's reporter role. This remake, as is the case with most redone film properties, was not in the same league as other screwball Hollywood comedies such as *Bringing Up Baby* (with Cary Grant and Katharine Hepburn), *My Man Godfrey* (with William Powell and Carole Lombard), Ann's earlier Frank Capra production of *You Can't Take It with You*, or the Spencer Tracy-Katharine Hepburn comedies.

In *Eve Knew Her Apples* Ann didn't dance a step, although she sang four numbers, including the hit song "I'll Remember April." Columbia gave Ann the same kind of star build-up which earlier had been given to Rita Hayworth. Miss Hayworth had also achieved fame for her dancing rather than for her acting. Appearances in motion pictures such as *Blood and Sand* and *Tales of Manhattan* later gave her the opportunity to prove her acting ability.

One of the songs in the film had been written by a sailor in the San Diego Naval Hospital, invalided from active service. "I've Waited a Lifetime" attracted the attention of Jay Gorney, a Columbia songwriter, and producer Irving Briskin who contacted Seaman Edward A. Brandt, R.H., 3/c, and arranged to use the song in *Eve Knew Her Apples*.

An interesting fan letter from an American GI arrived for Ann while she was working on this movie. The letter stated that a large pin-up photograph of her had been found on a wall in a captured German staff headquarters. It was the consensus of the cast and crew of *Eve Knew Her Apples* that the Germans had probably taken the photograph from an American soldier captured earlier.

Ann finished her Columbia years with third billing in *The Thrill of Brazil*. It was at this time that Ann fell in love with and married Reese Llewellyn Milner, heir to the Llewellyn Iron Works and Consolidated Steel Corporation, a company which also made Llewellyn elevators. Through mutual friends, Ann met Milner at a party at the Mocambo nightclub. Three months later, on February 16, 1946, they were married in Montecito, California.

Ann was in the process of filming *The Thrill of Brazil*, when Milner demanded that she give up her career. She was earning approximately $100,000 a year at Columbia, but Milner, a millionaire, was financially secure and felt his wife should not work. Ann told her boss, Harry Cohn, that when the picture was finished she was giving up her career to be Milner's wife. Cohn replied that she had a contract to fulfill but generously offered to shoot around her if the couple wanted to take a two-week honeymoon.

**With husband Reese Milner at
the reception following their wedding in Montecito.**

For *The Thrill of Brazil* Cohn had borrowed from M-G-M the services of director S. Sylvan Simon and star Keenan Wynn. In this film, Ann played the first of her "other woman" parts, the slot in which she eventually was placed at Metro. Ann's new image was chic and sophisticated, a departure from the demure wartime heroine of her former roles.

Eugene Loring staged Ann's big number, "Man Is Brother to a Mule." Ann danced continuously for six minutes, thirty-nine seconds, which added thirty-two seconds to her previous record. She also did 125 complete whirls, in itself some kind of record. Other numbers were "The Custom House," a Samba tap routine by Ann, and a Brazilian macumba, or voodoo dance, that featured Janet Collins, a soloist of the Katherine Dunham dance troupe. This voodoo dance was staged by Jack Cole with his assistant, Gwen Verdon, an unknown at this time. Allyn Joslyn (whom Keenan Wynn had understudied in the stage play *Boy Meets Girl*), Evelyn Keyes, and Tito Guizar were also in the cast. *Rendezvous in Rio* was the working title for the film.

Plans had been made for Ann's next feature. *The Petty Girl* was to have been her first major Technicolor musical for Columbia. But with Ann's marriage to Milner *The Petty Girl* was postponed, and before she completed filming *The Thrill of Brazil* she became pregnant. Production was delayed because of her pregnancy and an unhappy married life. Ann lost the baby, her marriage was over by November, and Cohn sued Milner for $150,000 for causing Ann to break her movie contract. Columbia eventually did make *The Petty Girl*, but not as a musical and not with Ann Miller. The 1950 Technicolor comedy starred Robert Cummings and Joan Caulfield.

Had Ann been able to forsee that her next job would be at Metro-Goldwyn-Mayer, cast in a spectacular motion picture musical opposite Judy Garland and Fred Astaire, being out of a job at Columbia wouldn't have seemed quite so tragic.

Ann tosses away her wedding bouquet as tradition warrants.

Linda Darnell was Ann's best friend. Ann was pregnant and the occasion was a luncheon and baby shower.

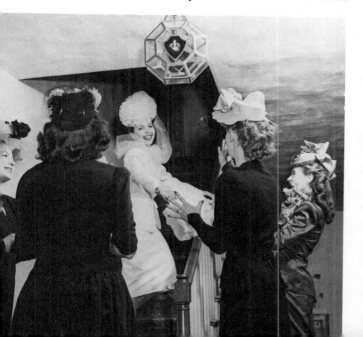

Release date: June 5, 1941

CAST

Daniel Collins	RUDY VALLEE
Kitty Brown	ANN MILLER
Frances Lewis	ROSEMARY LANE
Off-Beat Davis	ALLEN JENKINS
Joan Merrill	JOAN MERRILL
Mike Armstrong	RICHARD LANE
James Anderson	Stanley Andrews

Specialties
THE THREE STOOGES, BRENDA and COBINA,
SIX HITS and a MISS, EDDIE DURANT'S RHUMBA
ORCHESTRA, GLEN GRAY and HIS CASA LOMA BAND

"A Twiddlin' My Thumbs"   "Time Out for Rhythm"

"Time Out for Rhythm"

CREDITS

Director: Sidney Salkow *Producer*: Irving Starr *Screenplay*: Edmund L. Hartmann and Bert Lawrence *Story*: Bert Granet *Based on a play*: Alex Ruben *Assistant director*: Bud Brill *Director of musical numbers*: LeRoy Prinz *Musical director*: M. W. Stoloff *Director of Photography*: Franz F. Planer, A.S.C. *Art director*: Lionel Banks *Gowns*: Saltern *Sound recording*: P. J. Faulkner *Film editor*: Arthur Seid *Running time*: 75 minutes.

SONGS

Music and lyrics: Sammy Cahn and Saul Chaplin. "Time Out for Music," "A-Twiddlin' My Thumbs," "Obviously the Gentleman Prefers to Dance," "As If You Didn't Know," "The Boogie Woogie Man," "Rio De Janeiro," "Shows How Wrong a Gal Can Be."

SYNOPSIS

Nightclub singing star Frances Lewis (Rosemary Lane) decides to quit show business to be married. Her manager, Mike Armstrong (Richard Lane), who is in love with her, resents her decision.

Agent Danny Collins (Rudy Vallee) suggests that he and Mike go into partnership.

The booking agents are instantaneously successful with their first clients: Glen Gray and His Casa Loma Band, singer Joan Merrill, and the Six Hits and a Miss, whom they have booked for an important television show.

Frances, meanwhile, divorces her husband and returns to Mike wanting to go back into show business. Mike insists that Frances replace Joan on the telecast and can't understand Danny's animosity towards Frances.

Danny discovers Frances's maid Kitty Brown (Ann Miller) dancing and is impressed with her talent. Unknown to Mike, Danny and Off-Beat (Allen Jenkins), a piano player, rehearse Kitty for the starring role. When Mike discovers this deception he dissolves the partnership. Mike now engaged to Frances buys a nightclub in which to star his fiancée.

A Hollywood talent scout, Jim Anderson (Stanley Andrews), comes East to see Danny's new show. Danny appeals to Frances for the use of the club. The overly ambitious singer agrees but demands the star spot. Kitty disappears to give Danny his big chance.

When Mike asks Frances about the audition for the Hollywood agent she tells him that her career means more to her than anything or anybody. Mike, disillusioned, is furious and forbids her to appear in the show.

With Allen Jenkins and Rudy Vallee.

With Allen Jenkins: "Obviously the Gentleman Prefers to Dance."

Danny and Off-Beat hunt desperately for Kitty, who arrives in time to do the star number. Anderson offers everyone involved with the show Hollywood contracts. Mike and Danny resume their partnership.

CRITICAL REACTION

Bosley Crowther in the *New York Times:*
"Midsummer is no time to expect a knock-out musical picture, we know. But, on the basis of the title alone, one might have anticipated more from Columbia's *Time Out for Rhythm* than what one gets. But the truth of the matter is that this slight picture is a hopelessly heavy and labored attempt to entertain humorously and, except for the lovely and lively Miss Miller, who simply won't be suppressed, it has the distinction of being one of the dullest diversions in months. Miss Miller, when she sings or dances, does so charmingly and with ease. As musical pictures go, *Time Out for Rhythm* hits low C."

James Francis Crow in the *Hollywood Citizen-News:*
"*Time Out for Rhythm* is a painfully old-fashioned Hollywood musical show—corney is the word, I think—but I guess there are a lot of fans who are going to say that it is good enough for them. Rudy Vallee, Rosemary Lane, Allen Jenkins, Joan Merrill, and Richard Lane are among the assorted players present, but in this department it is Ann Miller's picture. She acts some and sings a bit, but most of all she dances—and, as they used to say, how! As the fans were saying after the preview last night she has the prettiest pair of legs in show business since Ann Pennington. For those who seek quantity rather than quality, it's a bargain."

Variety:
"Columbia tossed a carload of talent into this filmusical attempt with inauspicious results. Dragging story, combined with dull direction that fails to accentuate production numbers and songs, leaves things in a rather confusing state. Story never hits the line of credulity, and only the tap dance numbers of Ann Miller momentarily lift the onlooker out of slumping seats."

Wanda Hale in the *New York Daily News:*
"Speaking for the minority, which we hear is always right, we would say that Ann Miller's dancing is the picture's high spot. *Time Out for Rhythm* is a moderately entertaining musical. Sidney Salkow's direction of this Columbia musical is all right. He keeps it going at a pretty good pace and it's not his fault that the entertainers, excluding Miss Miller, are not tops." (Two and a half stars **½*)

GO WEST, YOUNG LADY

Release date: November 27, 1941

CAST

Belinda Pendergast	PENNY SINGLETON
Tex Miller	GLENN FORD
Lola	ANN MILLER
Jim Pendergast	Charlie RUGGLES
Hank	Allen JENKINS
Judge Harmon	Jed Prouty
Tom Hannegan	Onslow Stevens
Bob	Bob Wills
Mrs. Hinkle	Edith Meiser
Chief Big Thunder	Bill Hazlet
Waffles	Waffles

Specialties
THE FOURSOME, BOB WILLS
and HIS TEXAS PLAYBOYS

CREDITS

Director: Frank R. Strayer *Producer:* Robert Sparks *Screenplay:* Richard Flournoy, Karen DeWolf *Story:* Karen DeWolf *Assistant director:* Abby Berlin *Director of photography:* Henry Freulich, A.S.C. *Art director:* Lionel Banks *Costumes:* Walter Plunkett *Music recordings:* P. J. Faulkner *Musical director:* M. W. Stoloff *Assistant:* Paul Mertz *Dance director:* Louis DaPron *Film editor:* Gene Havlick *Running time:* 70 minutes.

SONGS

Music and lyrics: Sammy Cahn and Saul Chaplin. "Doggie, Take Your Time," "Gentlemen Don't Prefer a Lady," "I Wish That I Could Be a Singing Cowboy," "Rise to Arms," "Somewhere Along the Trail," "Go West, Young Lady;" "Ida Red" *lyrics and arrangement:* Bob Wills and His Texas Playboys.

SYNOPSIS

Jim Pendergast (Charlie Ruggles), owner of the Crystal Palace saloon in the frontier town of Headstone, learns that his nephew Bill is arriving on the next stagecoach. Pendergast thinks Bill will be the town's new sheriff. Headstone needs a sheriff because a mysterious masked bandit called Pecos Pete has been holding up the saloon.

When Bill arrives, "he" turns out to be Belinda Pendergast (Penny Singleton). But Belinda can take care of herself. Belinda helped Tex Miller (Glenn Ford), the new federal marshall, fight off Indians who attacked the stagecoach they were on.

Lola (Ann Miller), the star of the Crystal Palace, is jealous of Belinda when town banker Tom Hannegan (Onslow Stevens), Lola's boyfriend, shows an interest in the newcomer.

Pecos Pete again holds up the saloon just as Tex is proposing to Belinda. Pete escapes when Belinda throws a custard pie and hits Tex in the face. Pete removes his disguise in Lola's dressing room, revealing himself as Hannegan. Meanwhile Hank (Allen Jenkins) and Judge Harmon (Jed Prouty) have captured one of Hannegan's henchmen. Tex forms a posse and rides out to capture the renegades. Lola goes to warn Big Chief Thunder (Bill Hazlet) and to have the Indians ambush the posse on Hannegan's orders. Hannegan plans to loot the town while the men are away.

With Glenn Ford.

With Allen Jenkins: "I Wish That I Could Be a Singing Cowboy."

"Go West, Young Lady"

Belinda, feeling that she has only hindered Tex, prepares to leave Headstone. When she finds Pecos Pete's costumes in Lola's dressing room and suspects Hannegan of being the masked bandit, she fights with Lola. Belinda organizes the townswomen and sends one of the women to warn Tex. The women, armed with brooms, pots and pans, and rolling pins, ambush and subdue Hannegan and his men until Tex and the posse return to finish the job.

CRITICAL REACTION

Theodore Strauss
in the *New York Times:*
"Go West, Young Lady is like the clown's trunk —dig your hand into it and you're apt to come up with almost anything. Though most of the citizens of Headstone wear guns and spurs, don't let that confuse you into thinking that the film is strictly a Western; it's a musical and a slapstick comedy too. The brightest item by far is Ann Miller, the hectic little lady from Texas, who trips rhythmically across the bars of Headstone."

Kate Cameron in the
New York Daily News:
"Penny Singleton has at last broken away from the series she's been making for Columbia over the past couple of years. Penny plays the heroine of Go West, Young Lady with the same assurance that distinguished her impersonation of Blondie. At any rate, Penny and Glenn Ford, the latter as a quick-tempered sheriff, Ann Miller, as a dance hall artist, and Charlie Ruggles give this western opus a few extra licks of comedy. The girls add some spicy leg work in the stage entertainment sequences and contribute a face-slapping and hair-pulling contest that is well worth the price of admission. The picture is above the average western." (Two and a half stars **½*)

Variety:
"Go West, Young Lady is a slapstick, cowboy farce that generates numerous amusing moments. However, it will confuse horse opera fans if they take any of it too seriously. Main difficulty with entire story is that it wavers between usual standard cowboy heroics, chases and gunplay and the urge to go musical. The two never quite mesh. With Penny Singleton as the tomboy from the east who always gets her man, pitted against dance hall queen Ann Miller, trying to win the same man, a femme knockdown fight is in the cards. They make this bout thoroughly realistic. Miss Miller is unusually attractive as the dance hall entertainer although doing her specialty tapstering only briefly. Deserves a better break than being submerged in this subordinate role."

The *Hollywood Reporter:*
"Penny Singleton's first breakaway from the 'Blondie' series finds her cast in a rowdy Western burlesque with bandits, Injuns 'n' everything. She has the opportunity to sing and dance in Go West, Young Lady, and also stages a rough and tumble scrap with Ann Miller that is a dilly. An ace cast joins its vivacious star in giving lustre to the Sparks production. Glenn Ford plays his Texas sheriff for a hit, and the always pleasing Ann Miller shows her heels to the gang that pack the Crystal Palace. Louis DaPron served as dance director, and surprisingly Allen Jenkins does a hoofing routine with Miss Miller. Photography by Henry Freulich is of top quality for an outdoor opus."

Release date: March 21, 1942

CAST

Daisy Hawkins	JUDY CANOVA
Private Stephen Chandler	ALLAN JONES
Vicky Marlowe	ANN MILLER
Private J. Wethersby "Pinky" Fothergill	JERRY COLONNA
Sergeant Butts	William DEMAREST
Lieutenant Danvers	William WRIGHT
General Marlowe	Clarence KOLB
Private Dugan	Gordon JONES
Private O'Toole	Rod CAMERON
Drake	John MILJAN
Junior	Edward PAWLEY

Jerry Colonna, Judy Canova, Ann, and Allan Jones.

CREDITS

Director: Albert S. Rogell *Producer:* Sol C. Siegel *Associate producer:* Jules Schermer *Based on the novel* "She Loves Me Not" *by* Edward Hope *and a play by* Howard Lindsay *Screenplay:* Art Arthur, Bradford Ropes *Director of photography:* Daniel Fapp, A.S.C. *Adaptation:* Edmund Hartmann, Val Burton *Musical director:* Victor Young *Sound mixer:* Harry Mills *Art directors:* Hans Dreier, William Flannery *Film editor:* Alma Macrorie *Running time:* 77 minutes.

SONGS

Music and lyrics: Frank Loesser, Harold Spina; Joseph J. Lilley, Leo Robin, Ralph Rainger; Dorothy Fields, Jimmy McHugh. "Need I Speak?," "Jitterbug's Lullaby," "Spangle on My Tights," "In the Army," "Wacky for Khaki," "Swing in Line," "Love in Bloom," "I Can't Give You Anything But Love."

SYNOPSIS

The only eye-witness to the murder of a circus owner is the circus tight-rope walker Daisy Hawkins (Judy Canova). Daisy is being chased by both the hit-men who want to silence her, and by the police who want her to testify against the gangsters.

Daisy's sweetheart, J. Wethersby "Pinky" Fothergill (Jerry Colonna), is chief pigeon-trainer at a nearby army camp. Since Daisy doesn't know which way to turn, she hurries to Fothergill.

At the camp Private Stephen Chandler (Allan Jones) is rehearsing the big army show. Chandler mistakes Daisy as one of the boys in the chorus, thinking she looks like just another female impersonator. Fothergill tells Chandler the truth about Daisy. They both cut her hair and get her into uniform. Sergeant Butts (William Demarest) is convinced that Daisy is just one of the boys.

Vicky Marlowe (Ann Miller), daughter of the general (Clarence Kolb), becomes romantically interested in Chandler. The army show benefits because Vicky is a sensational tap dancer with real female legs.

Meanwhile, Daisy, who wins a medal for marksmanship, is a hit with the other soldiers and they insist on taking her to the town's night spot to celebrate. She is spotted there by the gangsters, who are still searching for her, when they see a "rookie" powdering her nose!

On the night of the big army show, Chandler plants police throughout the audience. The gangsters are all there to get Daisy.

However, Daisy is a crack shot. During the course of the show she disables each gangster, one by one, so that the police can take over and arrest each one of them. Chandler's army

With Allan Jones.

show is a big success and everyone is happy—everyone except the gangsters.

CRITICAL REACTION

Theodore Strauss in the New York Times:

"The fine art of tickling the public's rib is being practiced with all the consummate finesse of a longshoreman in *True to the Army*, Paramount's new patriotic posy at the Central. To be sure, young Ann Miller has a pair of miraculously nimble toes, Jerry Colonna has a nimble and occasionally comic mustache, and Allan Jones has a better than average tenor voice. As a comedy of errors, *True to the Army* is full of errors but no comedy. At present temperatures that should be emphatic enough."

Rose Pelswick in the New York Journal-American:

"In *True to the Army* there are hill-billy songs by Judy Canova, a romantic ballad by Allan Jones, some tap dancing by Ann Miller, and the typical Jerry Colonna brand of humor by Jerry Colonna. Knockabout farce set against the background of an Army camp, the rest is a collection of slapstick gags. Mr. Jones pops up as a Broadway star, now a private, who's staging a musical entertainment at the camp, and Miss Miller turns up as the Colonel's daughter. There are also the grumpy sergeant, the choleric Colonel and the song-and-dance numbers of the camp's musical show."

The Hollywood Reporter:

"*True to the Army* is an honestly wacky comedy, milked dry of laughs by the vigorous efforts of its cast and the punchy direction of Albert S. Rogell. Judy Canova and Jerry Colonna deliver antics as expected, both solidly. Allan Jones makes his Broadway producer personable, and Ann Miller dances with what the dialog allows is Phi Beta Tappa distinction. Wait until you hear her answer a machine gun with taps."

Variety:

"*True to the Army* should do well in most situations. It is better-than-average Paramount low-budget fare. Miss Canova is excellent in her usual hillbilly style, singing and dancing well and teaming nicely with Colonna to get most of the laughs. Ann Miller is standout with her dancing. What she lacks in Hollywood's stereotyped beauty standards she more than makes up for with some of the best hoofing seen in pictures. She does all right, too, in the romantic interludes with Jones and easily takes the honors from the rest of the cast. Jones is okay in his role and Colonna turns in a good performance."

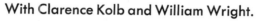

With Clarence Kolb and William Wright.

Release date: July 23, 1942

CAST

Donna D'Arcy	ANN MILLER
Lee Davis	BETTY RHODES
Jeep Jackson	JERRY COLONNA
Johnny Draper	JOHNNIE JOHNSTON
Mariposa Ginsbotham	VERA VAGUE
Harvey Erkimer	Harry Barris
Sticks O'Hara	Eddie Quillan
Push Gasper	Dave Willock
Cornetist	Nick Cochrane
Stage manager	Rod Cameron
E. V. Hartley	Arthur Loft

Specialty act	The Debonaires
Colonel Reeves	William Forrest
1st examiner	Warren Ashe
2nd examiner	Charles Halton
Jones	Lee Shumway

CREDITS

Director: Albert S. Rogell *Producer:* Sol C. Siegel *Original screenplay:* Art Arthur, Frank Loesser *Associate producer:* Burt Kelly *Photographer:* Daniel Fapp, A.S.C. *Musical director:* Victor Young *Art directors:* Hans Dreier, Haldane Douglas *Dance director:* Jack Donahue *Sound director:* Gene Merritt *Film editor:* Arthur Schmidt *Running time:* 79 minutes.

SONGS

Music and lyrics: Jule Styne, Herb Magidson, Frank Loesser. "Conchita, Marchita, Lolita, Pepita, Rosita, Juanita Lopez," "You're in Love with Someone Else," "I'd Love to Know You Better," "Cooperate with Your Air Raid Warden," "Here Comes Katrinka," "Payday."

SYNOPSIS

When Johnny Draper (Johnnie Johnston) and his band decide to take jobs at the Eagle Aircraft Company, Donna D'Arcy (Ann Miller), the band's singer and dancer, doesn't go along with the idea. Johnny's idea is that playing for the "swing shift" and improving plant morale will give the band national coverage. Donna takes a nightclub job, but intends to return when the band becomes famous.

Johnny becomes a student welder and Jeep Jackson (Jerry Colonna) becomes the hot dog and soft drink vender. There's trouble when Johnny meets his boss who treats him like a dunce. Johnny gets mad and is about to sock the guy when the boss removes his welding helmet and Johnny's boss is a girl, Lee Davis (Betty Rhodes). Johnny, hating female welders, gets transferred.

Ann rehearsing with the chorus boys.

Finale number.

The band, meanwhile, is getting national publicity. Bookers from New York and Chicago are beginning to become interested. At a swing shift dance, Johnny fails to recognize Lee. She is beautiful. He drives her home and, on the way, they stop off at the club where Donna is appearing. Donna introduces them. Her plan, though, to discredit Lee backfires. Lee, a former professional singer, sings Donna's hit song to the audience's approval.

Later at the plant, Johnny is rehearsing the big company show. He and Lee have the star spots while Jeep and his new girlfriend, Mariposa Ginsbotham (Vera Vague), handle the comedy. There is trouble backstage, for when Donna hears that a lot of bookers will be catching the show, she returns and takes over the top spot from Lee. Johnny convinces Lee that Donna is important for the show, but not in any other way.

The show is a hit and the band receives many offers. But Johnny and the boys reject the contracts and decide to stay at the plant working for Uncle Sam. Even Donna has a change of heart and stays on, too.

CRITICAL REACTION

Kate Cameron in the
New York Daily News:

"Ann Miller is the chief attraction at the Paramount Theatre this week, as she is playing one of the leading feminine roles in the picture, *Priorities on Parade*, and is the star attraction of the stage show. Ann has a clever pair of feet. She dances on the stage with and without music and never misses a beat. In the picture, she sings as well as she dances. She's gone blonde and has acquired a glamorous finish on her way up to stardom. In *Priorities on Parade*, which is a comedy with musical trimmings, Ann appears as a night club singer and dancer." (Two and a half stars **½*)

The *Hollywood Reporter*:

"*Priorities on Parade* is a very bright musical notion, solidly patriotic without striving to be. It is due to be hailed as morale-building entertainment and can hold its own at the box-office as a topline attraction. Betty Rhodes and Johnnie Johnson take premiere honors easily, yet Ann Miller makes her presence felt each time she unlimbers those amazing machine-gun taps. Her role of the overambitious dancer would have been a great deal more thankless in other hands. Direction by Albert S. Rogell sparks the light-hearted gayety of the affair, and he allows for no dull moments. The songs are uniformly first-rate. The production flash, 'Pay Day,' is smartly staged by Jack Donohue."

Theodore Strauss in
the *New York Times*:

"Despite occasional uproarious laughter, *Priorities on Parade* has the haphazard look of a musical comedy that was shot from the cuff. If ever it had a basic plot, it is practically unrecognizable now. The result is a running series of gags, songs and sketches that trip as often as they run. Ann Miller makes dextrous use of a spectacular pair of legs, but even that talent has its limits of enjoyment. As a morale builder *Priorities on Parade* has the tonic properties of a tall glass of lukewarm water."

Release date: February 4, 1943

CAST

Beverly Ross	ANN MILLER
Barry Lang	William WRIGHT
Andy Adams	Dick PURCELL
Vernon Lewis	Franklin Pangborn
Mr. Kennedy	Tim Ryan
Mrs. Ross	Barbara Brown
Eddie Ross	Larry Parks
Mr. Ross	Douglas Leavitt
Evelyn Ross	Adele Mara
Canvassback	Walter Sande
Stomp McCoy	Wally Vernon

Mr. Smith	Andrew Tombes
Elsie	Irene Ryan
Elmer	Doodles Weaver
Mrs. Browning	Virginia Sale
Laura Jean	Shirley Mills

Specialties

BOB CROSBY and HIS BAND, FREDDIE SLACK and HIS BAND with ELLA MAE MORSE, DUKE ELLINGTON and HIS BAND, COUNT BASIE and HIS BAND, FRANK SINATRA, MILLS BROTHERS, THE RADIO ROGUES

BITS

Medical officer Eddie Kane *Colonel Humphrey* Boyd Davis *Top sergeant* Eddy Chandler *Sergeant Anderson* Harry Anderson *Jenks* Si Jenks *Sentry* David Newell *Davis* Jack Rice *Director* John T. Murray *Announcer* Herbert Rawlinson *Mrs. Oliver* Jean Inness *Mr. Oliver* Ernest Hilliard *Maggie* Maude Eburne *Collins* Bobby Barber *Jackson* Eugene Jackson

CREDITS

Director: Charles Barton *Producer:* Sam White *Original screenplay:* Howard J. Green, Jack Henley, Albert Duffy *Assistant director:* Rex Bailey *Director of photography:* Philip Tannura, A.S.C. *Art director:* Lionel Banks *Associate:* Paul Murphy *Interior decorator:* Joseph

Kish *Technical radio adviser:* Jean Ruth *Musical director:* M. W. Stoloff *Sound engineer:* Jack Goodrich *Film editor:* James Sweeney *Running time:* 78 minutes.

SONGS

"Thumbs Up and V for Victory," "One O'Clock Jump," "Big Noise from Winnetka," "South Rampart Street Parade," "Take the A Train," "Cow-Cow-Boogie," "Cielito Lindo," "Night and Day," "Sweet Lucy Brown."

SYNOPSIS

Beverly Ross (Ann Miller), a switchboard operator at a Denver radio station, insists that a program of swing music would attract much attention. She manages, through a bit of subterfuge, to take over the early morning Vernon Lewis (Franklin Pangborn) classical music program. She substitutes jive music and dedicates the program to the servicemen in the area. Her 5:30 A.M. "Reveille with Beverly" radio show features swing music, bright chatter, and camp bulletins. It is an immediate success.

Eddie Ross (Larry Parks), Beverly's brother,

With Franklin Pangborn.

With Dick Purcell, Eddie Chandler, and William Wright.

is stationed at a nearby Army camp. He is overwhelmed when he hears the soldiers talking about his sister. Two of his buddies, Barry Lang (William Wright) and Andy Adams (Dick Purcell), want to meet Beverly, and Eddie arranges it. In civilian life, Andy was Barry's chauffeur. Andy feels that Barry stands a better chance with Beverly since he is wealthy. But Barry doesn't think this is true, so he swaps identities with his chauffeur.

Beverly likes them both. She tends to prefer Barry, although she believes Andy is a wealthy radio sponsor. When her brother tells her of their real identities, Beverly decides to have a little fun with her two ardent suitors.

During a personal appearance and radio broadcast at the camp, Beverly gets Barry and Andy to publicly admit to her who they really are.

After her big dance number, Beverly discovers that the auditorium is empty. The sol-diers have been given their orders to move—destination unknown. Beverly continues the show so that the radio audience won't suspect what has happened. She also sends a message to Barry and Andy that she likes them both and that she knew of their deception all along.

CRITICAL REACTION

The *Hollywood Reporter:*

"You can count the reasons *Reveille with Beverly* has become a sleeper success from Columbia, even if you are unable to count the taps of the picture's whirlwind dancing star, Ann Miller. The reasons are the musical interludes that allow a theatre to bill no less than four top-line dance bands plus the current rave vocalist, Frank Sinatra. The production by Sam White is a smooth-flowing natural, its direction by Charles Barton breezy and gay.

Ann Miller plays Beverly to score on abilities, apart from her dancing. In fact, she taps only in the finale, a breathless routine to the tune of 'Thumbs Up and V for Victory.' "

Kate Cameron in the
New York Daily News:

"Yehudi Menuhin, who has been entertaining the soldiers abroad with his virtuosity on the violin, recently gave an interview in which he said that the soldiers near the battlefronts prefer classical music to jazz. Ann Miller and her colleagues in *Reveille with Beverly* take the opposite view of the musical tastes of the boys in the American camps. *Reveille with Beverly* is a mildly amusing comedy from the Columbia studios. Ann Miller is given an opportunity to demonstrate her clever technique with taps in the last sequence of the picture and she is assisted in the plot sequences by William Wright and Dick Purcell, as a pair of rival suitors; Larry Parks, as her soldier brother;

Franklin Pangborn, as the impressario of the dawn program; and Barbara Brown and Douglass Leavitt, as her parents." (Two and a half stars **½*)

Daily Variety:

"Aimed to hit a certain audience known to be responsive to the kind of exciting music dished out by its collection of bands, *Reveille with Beverly* will fulfill its appointed mission with satisfaction, both as to its hearty comedy and its tune element. The pace is staccato, the music is representative of the various orchestras featured, and the laughs and entertainment are there. Ann Miller walks through her role until the final production number when she gets hot with a spirited hoofing routine in front of a line of servicemen for a camp show. Charles Barton directs his material with zest and pace. Production is handled ably by Sam White, gauging the entertainment intelligently for the intended patronage."

Ann was a star at the Denver Paramount!

"Thumbs Up and V for Victory"

WHAT'S BUZZIN' COUSIN?

Release date: July 8, 1943

CAST

Ann Crawford	ANN MILLER
Rochester	EDDIE "ROCHESTER" ANDERSON
Jimmy Ross	JOHN HUBBARD
Freddy Martin	Himself
Josie	Leslie BROOKS
Billie	Jeff DONNELL
May	Carol Hughes
Blossom	Theresa Harris
Jim Langford	Roy Gordon
Pete Hartley	Bradley Page
Dick Bennett	Warren Ashe

Jed . . . . Dub Taylor
Saree . . . . Betsy Gay
Hillbilly . . . . Louis Mason

And: FREDDY MARTIN and His Orchestra

CREDITS

Director: Charles Barton *Producer:* Jack Fier *Screenplay:* Harry Sauber *From a story by:* John P. Medbury *Assistant director:* Louis Germanprez *Director of photography:* Joseph Walker, A.S.C. *Art director:* Lionel Banks *Associate:* Paul Murphy *Set decorator:* Joseph Kish *Dance director:* Nick Castle *Musical director:* M. W. Stoloff *Sound engineer:* Lambert Day *Makeup artist:* Clay Campbell *Film editor:* James Sweeney *Running time:* 75 minutes.

SONGS

Music and lyrics: Walter Samuels, Saul Chaplin, Charles Newman, Lew Pollack, Don Raye, Gene de Paul, Jacques Press, Eddie Cherkose, Wally Anderson, Walter Donaldson, Mort Greene. "By Order of the Interceptor Command," "Three Little Mosquitoes," "In Grandpa's Beard," "They're Countin' in the Mountains," "Where am I Without You," "Ain't That Just Like a Man?," "Taffy," "Short, Fat and 4-F," "Knocked Out Nocturne," "Eighteen Seventy-Five," "Nevada."

SYNOPSIS

Ann Crawford (Ann Miller) has inherited the Palace Hotel and considerable surrounding property in a western ghost town. When Ann and her three friends, Josie (Leslie Brooks), Billie (Jeff Donnell), and May (Carol Hughes) arrive to claim her property, they find Freddy Martin, his band, and Rochester (Eddie Anderson) as unwilling guests at the hotel. The Martin band had been on a trailer vacation when they ran out of gas in the ghost town.

The four chorus girls pooled their savings in order to pay off the debts and they plan on running the hotel. Band singer Jimmy Ross (John Hubbard), using his own money, decides to help the girls fix the place up and turns the spot into a vacation hotel and nightclub.

Rochester, while digging in a victory garden he has started with his girlfriend, Blossom (Theresa Harris), finds a gold nugget. Word of a gold strike gets out. The rush is on, and the hotel does a thriving business.

Later, Pete Hartley (Bradley Page), a petty crook, arrives at the Palace with plans to get the property away from the girls. While Jimmy is away on business, and in spite of Ann's protests, the girls sell to Hartley. On his return, Jimmy thinks Ann has double-crossed him and they quarrel. The girls leave.

Jimmy later discovers that the gold nugget which Rochester found was only Rochester's own gold inlay. On a radio broadcast with Martin's band, Jimmy sings especially for Ann, hoping she will be listening. Jimmy finds that Ann is waiting for him at the conclusion of the program.

CRITICAL REACTION

A. H. Weiler in the *New York Times*: "Armed with a bulging dossier of songs and the services of Freddy Martin and his band, Ann Miller, and Eddie (Rochester) Anderson, Columbia's *What's Buzzin' Cousin?* is a minor musical tailored only to its featured players' dimensions. Miss Miller's dancing left nothing to be desired. . . . since there is no apparent connection between the title and the yarn, just what was it that was buzzin'?"

The *Hollywood Reporter*: "*What's Buzzin' Cousin?* is a question answered on the screen by the entertainment merits of Ann Miller's ace tap dancing, by Eddie (Rochester) Anderson's surefire clowning, and by the sweet, sweet music of Freddy Martin and his orchestra. Had they been backed up by something that approximated

With John Hubbard.

Leslie Brooks, Freddy Martin, Theresa Harris, Eddie Anderson,
Carol Hughes, Ann, John Hubbard, and Jeff Donnell.

a story, instead of the sorry excuse for a plot that was used, the Jack Fier production might have been hailed as a sleeper. While Miss Miller is dancing, Martin making with music and Rochester selling his laughs, the offering bounces with life. Direction by Charles Barton attempts to make the affair jell, as do a number of the players. All of which puts us right back where we started. *What's Buzzin' Cousin?* has Ann Miller, Eddie Anderson and Freddy Martin's music."

Kate Cameron in the
New York Daily News:
"Ann Miller, who has the shapeliest and most talented legs and feet on the screen, now that Eleanor Powell is bowing herself out of the M-G-M studios; Eddie Anderson, playing his favorite character of Rochester, and Freddy Martin's band are the chief attractions of *What's Buzzin' Cousin?* The title of the picture has no relation to anything seen or heard on Loew's State screen." (Two stars **)

"$18.75"

HEY, ROOKIE

Release date: April 6, 1944

CAST

Winnie Clark	ANN MILLER
Pendelton (Pudge) Pfeiffer	JOE BESSER
Jim Lighter	LARRY PARKS
Bert Pfeiffer	JIMMY LITTLE
Sergeant	Joe Sawyer
Colonel Robbins	Selmer Jackson
Captain Jessop	Larry Thompson
Mrs. Clark	Barbara Brown
General Willis	Charles Trowbridge
Sam Jonas	Charles Wilson
Corporal Trupp	Syd Saylor
Maxon	Doodles Weaver

With Barbara Brown.

Specialties

HI, LO, JACK AND THE DAME, CON-
DOS BROTHERS, THE VAGABONDS,
JOHNSON BROTHERS, JACK GILFORD,
JUDY CLARK and the SOLID SENDERS,
BOB EVANS with JERRY O'LEARY, The
HAL McINTYRE ORCHESTRA.

CREDITS

Director: Charles Barton *Producer*: Irving
Briskin *Screenplay*: Henry Myers, Edward El-
iscu, Jay Gorney *Based on the musical play by*:
E. B. (Zeke) Colvan, Doris Colvan *Title*,
"Hey, Rookie," originated by: John Percy
Hallowell Walker *Produced on the stage by*:
Original Yard Bird Club, Fort MacArthur, for
the benefit of the Athletic and Recreation
Fund, Fort MacArthur, California *Assistant
director*: Wilbur McGaugh *Associate produc-
ers*: Henry Myers, Edward Eliscu, Jay Gorney
Director of photography: L. W. O'Connell,
A.S.C. *Art director*: Lionel Banks *Associate*:
Rose Bellah *Set decorator*: Joseph Kish *Tech-
nical advisor*: Major Charles D. Sauvinet
Dance director: Val Raset *Music recording*:
Philip Faulkner *Musical director*: M. W. Sto-
loff *Sound engineer*: J. Haynes *Film editor*:
James Sweeney *Running Time*: 77 minutes

SONGS

Music and lyrics: Sergeant J. C. Lewis, Jr.,
Henry Myers, Edward Eliscu, Jay Gorney. "It's
Great to Be in Uniform," "There Goes Taps,"
"It's a Swelluva Life in the Army," "Take a
Chance," "When the Yard Birds Come to
Town," "Hey, Rookie," "Streamlined Sheik,"
"You're Good for My Morale," "Keep 'em
Happy," "He's Got a Wave in His Hair (and
a WAC on His Hands)," "American Boy,"
"So What Serenade."

SYNOPSIS

Jim Lighter (Larry Parks), a musical-comedy
producer, has joined the army to get away
from show business and from his former leading lady, Winnie Clark (Ann Miller).

Colonel Robbins (Selmer Jackson) wants
to put on an all-soldier show. Bert Pfeiffer
(Jimmy Little) tells him that a professional
producer is on the post and Lighter is given
the task of doing a show in three weeks on a
budget of $209. Winnie, star of the Broad-
way-bound musical *Step Lively*, gets a note
from Lighter telling her that he is doing a show
without her help.

During rehearsals, Lighter sees a newspaper notice about Winnie playing the army

With Selmer Jackson, Larry Parks, and Barbara Brown.

With Bill Shawn: "There Goes Taps."

"Streamlined Sheik"

With Larry Parks: "It's Good For My Morale."

post the next week to entertain the servicemen with numbers from her show.

Winnie, with the help of Pudge Pfeiffer (Joe Besser), does a torrid tap routine. The show is a hit with the soldiers. Afterwards the Colonel introduces his producer to Winnie and her mother (Barbara Brown). He tells Lighter that Winnie has offered her help with their show. Lighter accuses her of wanting to do it only for publicity, in order to advance her own career.

Winnie gives up her only free night to do volunteer work for the VAC's, a women's service organization. When Lighter sees her working unselfishly, he apologizes. They decide to do a preview of the show that very night.

The premiere of *Hey, Rookie* has to be moved up a few days to coincide with a visit from General Willis (Charles Trowbridge). It is performed for the first time after tactical maneuvers. The show is a hit. Winnie and Lighter are together once again as star and producer.

CRITICAL REACTION

Wanda Hale in
the *New York Daily News:*

"It sticks out all over that Columbia made *Hey, Rookie* on pocket change. Though, obviously inexpensive and unpretentious as it is, this soldier vaudeville show, with Ann Miller and Larry Parks, is fairly entertaining. *Hey, Rookie* presents its entertaining numbers like a vaudeville show. Ann Miller dances alone and sings and dances with Larry Parks. All in all, the show is pretty good, just about like one that would be put on in an Army camp. Of course, Miss Miller's dances are the most professional numbers and the best." (Two and a half stars **½*)

The *Hollywood Reporter:*

"In a good many respects, the stage show, *Hey, Rookie*, was more truly representative of the spirit of G.I. Joe than the lavishly spectacular *This Is the Army*. Producer Irving Briskin has been strikingly successful in giving it a film setting. Not done on the scale of the screen version of *This Is the Army*—something of a pity—it is, nevertheless, excellent fare which should score heavily at the box-office. The film includes most of the outstanding scenes of the stage show. It is to be regretted that the riotous GI fashion show of the stage offering does not appear in the film. On most other counts, it is a mighty good show. Ann Miller is brought into the situation logically and in addition to demonstrations of her tap virtuosity, gives a pleasing performance. The entertainment specialists, an imposing array, all are excellent. Charles Barton delivered a gratifying directorial effort which maintains a buoyant spirit and pace throughout."

JAM SESSION

Release date: April 13, 1944

CAST

Terry Baxter	ANN MILLER
George Carter Haven	Jess BARKER
Raymond Stuart	Charles D. Brown
Lloyd Marley	Eddie Kane
Berkley Bell	George Eldredge
Miss Tobin	Renie Riano
Henry	Clarence Muse
Evelyn	Pauline Drake
Coletti	Charles La Torre
Neva Cavendish	Anne Loos
Fred Wylie	Ray Walker

Specialties

Nan WYNN, THE PIED PIPERS, CHARLIE BARNET and HIS ORCHESTRA, ALVINO REY and HIS ORCHESTRA, LOUIS ARMSTRONG and HIS ORCHESTRA, JAN GARBER and HIS ORCHESTRA, GLEN GRAY and HIS CASA LOMA ORCHESTRA, TEDDY POWELL and HIS ORCHESTRA.

CREDITS

Director: Charles Barton *Producer:* Irving Briskin *Screenplay:* Manny Seff *From an original story by:* Harlan Ware, Patterson McNutt *Assistant director:* Earl Bellamy *Director of photography:* L. W. O'Connell, A.S.C. *Art directors:* Lionel Banks, Paul Murphy *Set decorator:* William Kiernan *Musical director:* M. W. Stoloff *Sound engineer:* Paul Holly *Film editor:* Richard Fantl *Running time:* 78 minutes.

SONGS

Music and lyrics: Jule Styne, Sammy Cahn. "Victory Polka," "Cherokee," "No Name Jive," "Brazil," "St. Louis Blues," "I Can't Give You Anything But Love," "I Lost My Sugar in Salt Lake City," "Murder He Says," "It Started All Over Again."

SYNOPSIS

The prize of a round-trip ticket to Hollywood has been won in a dance contest by Terry Baxter (Ann Miller). In the movie capital, the Kansas girl tries to get in to audition for the head of Superba Studios, Raymond Stuart (Charles D. Brown). Terry doesn't get a dancing job, but she does bluff her way into becoming a secretary to George Carter Haven (Jess Barker), a new writer who has been hired to write a screenplay for a movie entitled *Jam Session*. The studio has stipulated that George's

With Jess Barker.

With Charles D. Brown and Jess Barker.

"No Name Jive"

screenplay must include eight orchestras within the story.

George immediately likes Terry. When he is stuck for plot, Terry fills in with a story of her own. But Terry can't type what George has dictated. When she re-dictates it to a public stenographer, she thoroughly messes up George's screenplay. Stuart fires George when he reads the plot Terry has given him.

Terry, heartsick, tries to explain to Stuart what has happened. Again she can't get in to see him. Terry finally breaks into a Beverly Hills residence, thinking it belongs to Stuart. She is arrested and put in jail.

George and Stuart see her picture in the newspaper and both rush to her rescue. Terry ends up not only with a dancing part in George's new motion picture, but with George too.

CRITICAL REACTION

Paul P. Kennedy in the *New York Times:*
"Assigning a person addicted to normal socks and a one-piece suit to review an opus called *Jam Session* was painless even to the point of pleasurable. The Columbia picture which came to the Palace yesterday, starring Ann Miller with a flock of name bands, rolls evenly and amusingly along on an entertaining if somewhat pre-ration story. . . . the entire cast goes about its business to the tempo of light and smooth dialogue. Ann Miller, pretty and competent, sparks, as she should, the show, winding up in a production of 'Victory Polka.' "

Wanda Hale in the *New York Daily News:*
"*Jam Session*, starring Ann Miller and featuring six name bands, might be called a middle-class musical comedy, one which falls in entertainment value between the Technicolor extravaganzas and the budget musicals that are cluttered up with second-rate talent. It's a natural for the young folks. And it won't be hard for the adults to bear. This Columbia production has a good foundation, a story that has sufficient originality to see it through. Miss Miller proves to be a talented comedienne as well as a skilled dancer. Until the last, she plays a straight role, then she dances beautifully. Capable players support her and Charles Barton has directed the picture with a great deal of care. The music is worked into the plot in a pleasingly unique manner." (Three stars ***)

Variety:
"*Jam Session* merely furnishes band music to please the hepcats and, on the strength of its six bands, should fit into the nabe dualers. Ann Miller does well in the finale dance routine and attempts to inject interest in the trivial plot, while Jess Barker is likeable and pleasing as the brash writer. Rest of the cast [is] adequate."

"No Name Jive"

With Bill Shawn: "Victory Polka."

CAROLINA BLUES

Release date: December 20, 1944

CAST

Kay Kyser . . . . KAY KYSER
Julie Carver . . . . ANN MILLER
Phineas, Elliott, Hiram, Horatio,
      Aunt Martha, Aunt Minerva Carver . . . . . VICTOR MOORE
Charlotte Barton . . . . Jeff DONNELL
Georgia Carroll . . . . Georgia CARROLL
Ish Kabibble . . . . M. A. BOGUE
Harry Babbitt . . . . Harry BABBITT
Sully Mason . . . . Sully MASON
Diana . . . . Diana PENDLETON
Tom Gordon . . . . Howard Freeman

Roland Frisby	Robert Williams
Skinny	Doodles Weaver
Maisie	Dorothea Kent
Cab driver	Frank Orth
Eddie	Eddie Acuff

Specialties
HAROLD NICHOLAS, JUNE RICH-
MOND, THE CRISTIANIS, THE LAY-
SON BROTHERS, THE FOUR STEP
BROTHERS, KAY KYSER'S BAND

CREDITS

Director: Leigh Jason *Producer:* Samuel
Bischoff *Screenplay:* Joseph Hoffman, Al Martin *Story:* M. M. Musselman, Kenneth Earl
Additional dialogue: Jack Henley *Assistant director:* Ray Nazarro *Director of photography:*
Franz F. Planer, A.S.C. *Camera operator:*
George Kelly *Art directors:* Lionel Banks, Edward Jewell *Set decorator:* Joseph Kish *Music recording:* William Randall *Gowns:* Jean
Louis *Jewels:* Hobe *Musical direction:* M. W.
Stoloff *Dances:* Sammy Lee *Orchestral arrangements:* George Duning *Vocal arrangements:* Saul Chaplin *Sound engineer:* John
Goodrich *Film editor:* James Sweeney *Running time:* 81 minutes.

SONGS

Music and lyrics: Jule Styne, Sammy Cahn,
Dudley Brooks, Walter Bullock. "There Goes
That Song Again," "You Make Me Dream
Too Much," "Thanks a Lot," "Poor Little
Rhode Island," "Mr. Beebe," "Thinkin'
About the Wabash."

SYNOPSIS

Kay Kyser and his band, returning from entertaining servicemen overseas, decide to take a
much-needed vacation. Kyser's featured soloist, Georgia Carroll, announces that she is
quitting the band to get married. However,
Kyser's publicist, Charlotte Barton (Jeff Donnell), has promised Phineas J. Carver (Victor
Moore) that the band will do a show for the
workers at the Carver Defense Plant. Phineas
pretends to be one of the wealthy Carvers in
order to get his daughter, Julie (Ann Miller),
a job with Kyser's band. Kyser likes Julie's
voice, but because he feels that rich girls are
insincere and unreliable he refuses to hire her.

Tom Gordon (Howard Freeman), who
lives in Kyser's hometown, tries to get the
bandleader to stage a bond rally in Rocky
Mount, North Carolina, in order to raise
money for a battle cruiser to be named after
their town. Instead, Kyser stages the show in
New York. Georgia arranges for Julie to sing
in her place. Kyser is furious and still refuses
to hire Julie on a permanent basis.

Later, in Rocky Mount, Kyser gets govern-
ment notification that the money which was
raised in New York cannot be allocated to another section of the country. In order to stage
another rally, Kyser sends his vacationing
band members telegrams stating that he is
dying.

Phineas and Julie also arrive in Rocky
Mount. Since Kyser thinks he can get a lot
of money out of Phineas, he starts seeing a
lot of them both. Kyser falls in love with Julie.
Phineas rounds up his rich relatives and shakes
them down for twenty million dollars, thus
making the rally a huge success. The *U.S.S.
Rocky Mount* is now a reality. Julie finally
becomes permanent both in Kyser's life and
on the bandstand.

CRITICAL REACTION

Bosley Crowther in the *New York Times:*
"The so-called pride of Rocky Mount, N.C.,
Kay Kyser, is advertising himself and his
home town in Columbia's so-called musical
picture, *Carolina Blues.* And the way he is doing it this time is by playing at leading his
band in a series of war-bond rallies to raise
money for a cruiser, Rocky Mount. As the
prop for these musical sessions there is non-

With Kay Kyser.

With Kay Kyser: "Mr. Beebe."

The entire cast of *Carolina Blues.*

sense which passes for a plot wherein Victor Moore and Ann Miller pursue Mr. Kyser in search of a job. And that is *Carolina Blues,* neighbors. It is likely to leave you depressed. Miss Miller is virtually brushed off as the lady pursuing Mr. Kyser. One song number, 'Mr. Beebe,' done by Harold Nicholas and a Negro troupe, rates a high grade for peppiness and satire. And 'There Goes That Song Again' is good. But the rest—well, they're on the same order as the picture, which is pretty grim."

The *Hollywood Reporter:*

"For *Carolina Blues,* Columbia assembled a large array of talent, including some important names. This talent gives out right lustily and without stint throughout the picture. A couple of the songs are good and the band numbers are very hot indeed. Upon the foregoing combination the boxoffice future of the film depends, with the draw of Kay Kyser, Ann Miller, and Victor Moore promising to give it considerable impetus. In all honesty, however, it must be admitted that the quality of the picture fails to measure up to the standard of its individual performers. Kay Kyser handles his semi-romantic role nicely but he is even better as a band leader. Ann Miller looks lovely and performs well but her magic feet, than whose none are nimbler, are allowed

to twinkle in only one routine, for some incomprehensible reason. Instead, she sings twice, and rather well. The acting honors are corralled by Victor Moore."

Kate Cameron in the *New York Daily News:*

"With Kay Kyser and his band on the screen and Milt Britton and his screwy crew on the stage, the program at Loew's State Theater this week is given over to low gags and jivey tunes. *Carolina Blues* is blessed with the presence of Kay's gorgeous bride, Georgia Carroll, Ann Miller and her twinkling toes, and Jeff Donnell's droll comedy, on the distaff side, and with Victor Moore as the extra, added gagman. Kyser's part in the film is not in the best of taste. His camp and bond-selling tours are made the basis of the story and thoroughly exploited in Kyser's favor. Victor Moore has a few amusing moments in the film; Ann Miller does a dance number expertly and Georgia Carroll, Ann and Harry Babbitt put over the vocal numbers of the film. 'Mr. Beebe,' a satire on New York columnist Lucius Beebe's sartorial elegance, is made the subject of a lavish production number that is danced by Harold Nicholas and sung by the Layson Brothers, against a Lenox Avenue background. This is one of the funniest and liveliest spots in the picture." (Two and a half stars **½*)

EADIE WAS a LADY

Release date: January 23, 1945

CAST

Eadie Allen/Edithea Alden . . . . ANN MILLER
Professor Diogenes Dingle . . . . JOE BESSER
Tommy Foley . . . . William WRIGHT
Pamela (Pepper) Parker . . . . Jeff DONNELL
Jim Tuttle . . . . Jimmy LITTLE
Hannegan . . . . Tommy Dugan
Rose Allure . . . . Marion Martin
Aunt Priscilla Alden . . . . Kathleen Howard
Caleb Van Horne, VIII . . . . George Meeker
Reverend Ames . . . . George Lessey
Maid . . . . Ida Moore

Specialty dancer . . . . Jack Cole
Dean Flint . . . . Douglas Wood

And: HAL McINTYRE
and HIS ORCHESTRA

CREDITS

Director: Arthur Dreifuss *Producer*: Michel Kraike *Original story and screenplay*: Monte Brice *Assistant director*: Ray Nazarro *Director of photography*: Burnett Guffey, A.S.C. *Art director*: Carl Anderson *Set decorator*: Louis Diage *Orchestrations*: George Duning *Musical director*: M. W. Stoloff *Dance director*: Jack Cole *Sound engineer*: Ed Bernds *Film editor*: James Sweeney *Running time*: 67 minutes.

SONGS

Music and lyrics: Saul Chaplin, Sammy Cahn, Phil Moore, L. Wolfe Gilbert, Ben Oakland, Howard Gibeling, Harold Dickinson, Buddy De Sylva, Nacio Herb Brown. " 'Til You Came Along," "Eadie's Back," "I'm Gonna See My Baby," "Gypsy from Brooklyn," "Tabby the Cat," "Eadie Was a Lady."

SYNOPSIS

Boston debutante Edithea Alden (Ann Miller) is leading a double life. She is a proper college girl by day and Eadie Allen, a dancer in *Foley's Jollities Burlesque*, by night. When star Rose Allure (Marion Martin) fails to draw customers, owner Tommy Foley (William Wright) offers Eadie a dramatic bit in the show.

Meanwhile, preparations are being made at the college for a Greek festival. The Dean hires two former burlesque comics, Professor Diogenes Dingle (Joe Besser) and Jim Tuttle (Jimmy Little) to stage the pretentious dance. Eadie and her roommate, Pamela Parker (Jeff Donnell), are in the show.

Eadie's ambition is to become a dramatic actress, but the first skit she does at the *Jollities* ends with her getting hit in the face with a cake. An old lady at the stage door, paid

off by Tommy, cons Eadie into staying. The customers like Eadie and her star rises. Rose Allure gets a phony telegram with a better job offer, and she quits. Eadie is now the star attraction. Tommy wants to build a big publicity campaign for Eadie so that he can produce a Broadway show around her.

At *The Glass Slipper* nightclub, bandleader Hal McIntyre introduces Eadie. She is afraid of the publicity and rushes out, leaving Tommy and her job. The Dean and his wife, celebrating their anniversary at the club, do not recognize her. With Eadie gone, the *Jollities* is forced to close.

An agent offers Tommy the job of staging a benefit show with Eadie. Tommy finally discovers who she really is and confronts her at her sorority house. Eadie relents and agrees to do the benefit so that Tommy can line up backers for the proposed Broadway production.

When Rose Allure finds out her job offer was phony, she sends the police to raid the benefit. Eadie thinks Tommy has staged the raid as a publicity stunt, but he gets Rose to confess that it was her idea.

The college board decides to expell Edithea because of the scandalous publicity. Tommy, in the disguise of a phony professor, gets the board to reverse their decision. He tells them that Eadie was only helping him research a thesis on classical arts benefiting from modern theater. The "professor" stages the college festival, now titled *The Greeks Never Mentioned It*. Aunt Priscilla (Kathleen Howard) gives her blessing to the romance of Eadie and Tommy.

CRITICAL REACTION

Kate Cameron in the
New York Sunday News:

"Columbia has taken the song that Ethel Merman popularized some years ago, 'Eadie Was a Lady,' [and] used it as title and theme song for a film comedy that is now being shown at the Albee Theater in Brooklyn. Ann Miller is the bright, particular star of the Columbia comedy and if it weren't for her expertness in putting over the theme song, as well as several other tunes and a dance number or two, this bit of musical burlesque would scarcely be worth the time it takes to show it. Miss Miller is a capable and attractive entertainer and deserves better by Columbia than the quickies she's been assigned to. She has served her apprenticeship in the Bs and the Cs and we'd like to see her blossom into an A star some day.

William Wright, Jeff Donnell, Tommy Dugan, Marion Martin and the Hal McIntyre orchestra do their best to liven this mediocre musical burlesque, but only Ann Miller's contributions in the way of song and dance raise it above the level of low, cheap comedy." (Two stars **)

"Til You Came Along"

"Eadie Was a Lady" with Hal McIntyre and Orchestra.

Variety:

"That *Eadie Was a Lady* is a fairly entertaining, well produced supporting feature is largely due to Ann Miller and Joe Besser. Nicely-paced direction of Arthur Dreifus also helps pull it from the mire of implausibilities. Miss Miller does a slick job singing. 'Eadie' is given plenty of production and is the best tune in the film. Miss Miller cleans up with her deft tapstering as usual."

The *Hollywood Reporter:*

"*Eadie Was a Lady* gives personable Ann Miller an opportunity to sing and dance a sultry version of the song from which the title was adapted—complete with Mae West flourishes. But beyond the very likeable presence of the star, *Eadie* is not much of a show. Honors easily go to Ann Miller who troops through an inane part with commendable perseverance. When given an opportunity to dance and display her shapely torso, Miss Miller demonstrates anew that she is worthy of more auspicious vehicles."

With choreographer Jack Cole.   "I'm Gonna See My Baby"

Finale: "The Greeks Never Mentioned It."

EVE KNEW HER APPLES

Release date: April 12, 1945

CAST

Eve Porter . . . . ANN MILLER
Ward Williams . . . . William WRIGHT
Steve Ormand . . . . Robert WILLIAMS
George McGrew . . . . Ray WALKER
Joe Gordon . . . . Charles D. Brown
Walter W. Walters, II . . . . John Eldredge
Roberts . . . . Eddie Bruce
Doctor . . . . Frank Jaquet

With Robert Williams and Ray Walker.   With Robert Williams, William Wright, and Ray Walker.

"I'll Remember April"

BITS

Maid Betty Hill *Mrs. Green* Jessie Arnold *Mr. Birch* Boyd Davis *Wrestler* Abe Dinovitch *1st officer on motorcycle* Al Hill *2nd officer on motorcycle* Syd Saylor *Janice* Mary Rowland *Matron of Honor* Alemeda Fowler *Landlord* Si Jenks *Mr. Green* Hank Bell *Sheriff* Dick Rush *Landlady* Minta Durfee *Hotel clerk* Jack Rice *Announcer* Tom Hanlon *Toni* Harry Semels *Reporter* John Tyrrell *Rewrite men* George Ford, Dick Thorne

CREDITS

Director: Will Jason *Producer*: Wallace Mac-Donald *Screenplay*: E. Edwin Moran *Story*: Rian James *Assistant director*: Ray Nazarro *Director of photography*: Burnett Guffey *Art director*: Carl Anderson *Set decorator*: Louis Diage *Sound engineer*: H. Fogetti *Dialogue director*: Monte Collins *Film editor*: Jerome Thoms *Running time*: 64 minutes.

SONGS

Music and lyrics: Jimmy Kennedy, Edward Brandt, Bob Warren, Don Raye, Gene dePaul Pat Johnston. "An Hour Never Passes," "I've Waited a Lifetime," "Someone to Love," "I'll Remember April." "Vita-Vim Flakes Calypso Song," *written and sung by*: Sir Lancelot.

SYNOPSIS

Eve Porter (Ann Miller), Continental Broadcasting singing star, wants a thirteen-week rest after her fifth season. George McGrew (Ray Walker), her manager, and Steve Ormand (Robert Williams), her press agent, try to dissuade her with promises of a motion picture contract from Emperor Pictures and a personal appearance tour, but Eve leaves for Las Vegas right after the broadcast. She travels by bus to avoid being recognized, but the other passengers soon discover her identity.

McGrew and Ormand follow her to Las Vegas. To avoid them, Eve takes refuge in the trunk of the first car she sees. The car belongs to Ward Williams (William Wright), a reporter for the *Los Angeles Bulletin*.

Williams overhears that the highway police are looking for escaped murderess Edith Palmer, tagged the "canary widow" because she sings to her victims. Eve, snugly tucked away in the trunk, doesn't hear about the dragnet. When she reveals herself to Williams, he thinks she is the murderess.

Thinking he can deliver a scoop for his newspaper, Williams asks his editor Joe Gordon (Charles D. Brown) for a thousand-dollar fee for the story and the stipulation that he can't be fired for sixty days. He takes Eve to a motel for the night. Meanwhile, McGrew has offered a reward for information regarding Eve's disappearance.

Williams thinks Eve is trying to poison him the next morning as he hears her singing while fixing breakfast. Eve is recognized by Roberts (Eddie Bruce), a motel guest, who tries to cut himself in for the reward. Williams pretends to be a gangster kidnapping Eve and scares off the would-be blackmailer.

Eve, in love with Williams, finally convinces him of her true identity, and he takes her back to Hollywood. Staying off the main highway, they spend the night in a hayfield. During the night, while she sleeps, Williams drives to the city and writes their love story for the same thousand dollars so they can be married.

In the morning a farmer's wife turns Eve over to the sheriff. Eve calls her manager and decides to marry her stuffy fiancée, Walter W. Walters, II (John Eldredge). William's story is now worthless, and he returns the money.

On Eve's wedding day McGrew gets a letter from William asking to see him on a financial matter. Eve tells her agent to pay off the reporter, thinking he wants the reward. However, Williams produces an itemized bill for the expenses he incurred while Eve was with him. The total cost is $35.10. Williams tells McGrew that he loves Eve. When McGrew relates this to Eve, she runs out on her wedding and hides again in Williams's car trunk. When he sees Eve this time, she is in her wedding dress.

With William Wright.

CRITICAL REACTION

Variety:

"Ann Miller's singing and William Wright's acting help put this item into the class of an acceptable dualler. Miss Miller does four songs. One of them, 'Someone to Love,' by Bob Warren, makes for swell listening, and the others are done pleasantly too. Production is decidedly on the nether side of the budget. But Wright and Miss Miller are good, as far as script and business at hand will let them."

Wanda Hale in the *New York Daily News:*

"Many succeeding comedies have been influenced by *It Happened One Night,* but never before has a comedy borne such a bold resemblance to the Gable-Colbert film as *Eve Knew Her Apples.* Columbia produced both pictures so I guess the great likeness is legitimate. While *Eve Knew Her Apples* is not a carbon copy of *It Happened One Night,* it's so much like it in the second half that it's downright funny. In the course of events, Miss Miller bursts into song several times, and pleasingly, too." (Two stars **)

Daily Variety

"*Eve Knew Her Apples* could be sub-titled *It Happened One Night,* but isn't intended to duplicate the success of that Academy Awards winner. Aimed for slotting as a program musical, *Eve* will serve okay in that classification. Production gets the most values for the budget and direction keeps things moving. Ann Miller is spotlighted with five songs, but does not dance. Tunes are good and her comedy playing neatly presented. William Wright does well by the reporter assignment. Production guidance of Wallace MacDonald marshals workmanlike technical factors, including photography by Burnett Guffey and others."

Release date: September 30, 1946

CAST

Vicki Dean	EVELYN KEYES
Steve Farraugh	KEENAN WYNN
Linda Lorens	ANN MILLER
John Harbour	ALLYN JOSLYN
Tito Guizar	TITO GUIZAR
Veloz and Yolanda	VELOZ AND YOLANDA
Ludwig Kriegspiel	Felix Bressart
Irkie Bowers	Sid Tomack
Luiz	Eugene Borden
Dance soloist	Janet Collins

And: ENRIC MADRIGUERA and HIS ORCHESTRA

BITS

Bartender George J. Lewis *Show girls* Mary Meade, Norma Brown, Helen Chapman *Primitive drummer* J. Emanuel Vanderhauf *Specialty dancers* Edward Lynn, Onset (Tom-Tom) Conley *Stage manager* Pat Lane *Show girls* Diane Mumby, Jasmin Jenks, Peggy Maley, Doris Houck, Nita Mathews, Cornelia Kirwin, Daun Kennedy *Little man* Eddie Parkes *Bit policeman* Jamiel Hasson *Cafe manager* Antonio Filauri *Waiter* Robert Conte *Pedrina* Nino Bellini *Alberto* Martin Garralaga *Head waiter* Fred Godoy *Night clerk* Leon Lenoir *Bit policeman* Manuel Paris *Hotel Clerk* John Laurenz *Policeman* Joe Dominguez *Car driver* Alex Montoya *Photographer* Frank Yaconelli *Porter* Antonio Roux *Ticket taker* Paul Monte *Bits* John Fostini, George Mendoza, Nina Bara

CREDITS

Director: S. Sylvan Simon *Producer:* Sidney Biddell *Screenplay:* Allen Rivkin, Harry Clork, Devery Freeman *Assistant directors* James Nicholson, Earl McEvoy *Director of photography:* Charles Lawton, Jr., A.S.C. *Camera operator:* Victor Scheurich *Art directors:* Stephen Goosson, Van Nest Polglase, A. Leslie Thomas *Set decorators:* James M. Crowe, Robert Priestley *Makeup:* Clay Campbell *Hair styles:* Helen Hunt *Sound engineer:* Jack Haynes *Musical recording:* Philip Faulkner *Gowns:* Jean Louis *Dance directors:* Jack Cole, Eugene Loring, Nick Castle *Orchestrations/Musical director:* Leo Arnaud *Assistant:* Paul Mertz *Vocal arrangements:* Saul Chaplin *Technical adviser:* Louis Oliveira *Film editor:* Charles Nelson *Running time:* 91 minutes.

SONGS

Music and lyrics: Allan Roberts, Doris Fisher, Raphael Duchesne, Enric Madriguera, Albert Gamse. "The Custom House," "Man Is Brother to a Mule," "The Thrill of Brazil," "Silhouette Samba," "My Sleepy Guitar," "Copa Cabana," "Linda Mujer (You Never Say Yes and You Never Say No)," "Minute Samba," "Mucho Dinero."

SYNOPSIS

Steve Farraugh (Keenan Wynn), manager and revue-producer of Rio de Janeiro's posh Hotel Carioca, is still in love with his ex-wife, Vicki Dean (Evelyn Keyes). Nightclub star Linda Lorens (Ann Miller) is in love with Steve, and singer Tito Guizar is in love with Linda.

Vicki, accompanied by her fiancée John Harbour (Allyn Joslyn), president of the Pearly Dent Toothpaste Company, comes to Rio to get Steve's signature on the final divorce papers. Steve had previously signed the papers with disappearing ink. This time Vicki makes Steve use John's pen. When John puts the papers in his wallet, he inadvertently exchanges pens with Steve. Steve still hopes to win Vicki back. He asks his ex-wife, a famous dance director, to stay and restage the finale of his new show.

Steve also asks Irkie Bowers (Sid Tomak), a cab driver, to steal John's wallet. Since Irkie knows that Steve's pen is filled with disappearing ink, he takes John's pen for Steve to sign Irkie's check for his work. When Irkie is unable to cash the check he tells Linda about the theft of the wallet. Steve, seeing Rio with Vicki and John, manages to get his wallet back. Linda and Irkie arrive with the police, who take the group to jail.

Steve is able to bail them out but plants newspaper photographers to take pictures of John when they are released. John fears the scandal will ruin a pending deal with an Argentine firm, so he flies to Buenos Aires. Linda then gets the wallet from Steve and gives it to Vicki.

Steve confesses that he is still in love with Vicki. He then discovers that Vicki didn't need a new signature on the divorce papers. Lemon juice could have been used to bring out the first signature. Vicki has simply stayed in Rio just to be with him.

"The Custom House"

"Man Is a Brother to a Mule"

With Allyn Joslyn, Keenan Wynn, and Evelyn Keyes.

CRITICAL REACTION

The *Hollywood Reporter:*

"Few audiences will fail to recognize this latest dodge to use *The Front Page* plot for a picture. Unfortunately in re-plating *Front Page* in this musical manner producer Sidney Biddell hasn't provided it with more than a single joke. The revue sequences have some interesting dances staged by Eugene Loring and Nick Castle. Ann Miller does some of her best tapping. Sometimes the screen is over-crowded with dancing figures, but such circumstances are seldom criticized."

Wanda Hale in the *New York Daily News:*

"Dancing is the keynote of Loew's State Theater's new program. On the screen, *The Thrill of Brazil* features, Ann Miller, Veloz and Yolanda, and South American dances that are original and interesting. *The Thrill of Brazil*, by Columbia, has Keenan Wynn, Evelyn Keyes, and Allyn Joslyn in the comedy roles while the entertainment is handled by the dancers, Tito Guizar, singing, and Enric Madriguera's orchestra and singer. With all this talent and the handsome South American settings, *The Thrill of Brazil* is just another Hollywood musical comedy." (Three stars ***)

Daily Variety:

"Columbia has a money picture on its hands in *The Thrill of Brazil*, a hit musical from the word go. Film is produced lavishly, packed with melodic song and colorful dancing numbers. Against this background is woven catchy songs by Ann Miller and Tito Guizar, dances featuring Miss Miller and large choruses. As staged by Eugene Loring and Nick Castle, these dances, most carrying South American motifs and the outstanding number of Voodoo extraction, merit attention and praise and provide something different in the way of entertainment. Ann Miller's singing and dancing are tops, and gives an impressive account of herself as star of the revue."

Thomas M. Pryor in the *New York Times*:
"The gentlemen who did the script for *The Thrill of Brazil* must have labored under the misapprehension that a bit of humor would be out of place in a romantic comedy liberally garnished with music and dancing. The thin story thread is buffeted about at considerable length and is relieved at intervals by the dancing of Veloz and Yolanda, the singing of Tito Guizar, a thoroughly diverting rendition of 'Minute Samba' by Enric Madriguera and orchestra and a sprightly song and dance interlude by Ann Miller. And there are a couple of flashy production numbers, which smack more of tired Hollywood choreography than Brazilian folk ways. S. Sylvan Simon's direction is wily enough to give the picture a sense of pace, but one can't help feeling that the players, for all their swift moving about, just don't get anywhere or do anything that is more than passably diverting at best."

The *Film Daily*:
"S. Sylvan Simon has directed *The Thrill of Brazil* with a fine eye for visual appeal which is evident all the way in production numbers. Music, dancing and kindred angles are done with a fine, tasteful flair which suitably drape about the framework of comic plot. There's Ann Miller's first rate dancing. The screenplay is mature fun, musical and an all-round pleasant good thing."

The Thrill of Brazil finale.

THE M-G-M YEARS

Ann Miller's performance in Columbia's *Eadie Was a Lady* not only captivated the critics but enchanted the head of the Metro-Goldwyn-Mayer studios, Louis B. Mayer. On the strength of her performance in this "B" musical, Mayer offered Ann a chance in the major leagues with a test for *Easter Parade*.

M-G-M's motto was "more stars than there are in heaven"—but Mayer's tap dancing star, Eleanor Powell, retired at the peak of her career when she married Glenn Ford, Ann's co-star in Columbia's *Go West, Young Lady*. M-G-M had dancers such as Cyd Charisse, Vera-Ellen and Lucille Bremer under contract, but no whirlwind tap dancer. Mayer was also smart enough to realize that Ann should be working for M-G-M and not competing with their musical product at another studio. Ann also resembled songstress Ginny Simms, a favorite of Mayer's. So after *Easter Parade* in 1948 Ann signed with Metro-Goldwyn-Mayer and began the third phase of her movie career.

Ann has said that if she had not moved to M-G-M and stayed at Columbia, she would have remained in the Jeff Donnell class—a name to be remembered by only the movie buff, but not by the general public.

The movie audience's first look at M-G-M's new dancing star was in Irving Berlin's *Easter Parade*. This was the first time that Ann was photographed in Technicolor.

M-G-M liked movie "teams" such as Jeanette MacDonald and Nelson Eddy; Spencer Tracy and Katharine Hepburn; and Judy Garland and

Gene Kelly, who had worked well together in *For Me and My Gal* and *The Pirate*. The pair was scheduled to start work in *Easter Parade*, along with Cyd Charisse and Peter Lawford, but during the month-long rehearsal period Kelly broke his ankle and had to withdraw from the picture. Fred Astaire had reportedly "retired," but producer Arthur Freed persuaded him to step in and replace Kelly, who would be incapacitated for six to eight months.

Cyd Charisse then pulled a tendon in her leg and couldn't work in the movie. Mayer helped arrange for Ann to test with Freed for Cyd's role of "Nadine Hale." Though she was one of many tested, Ann won the role. (While Ann was still at Columbia she had dated Mayer, along with many of Hollywood's eligible bachelors, but it was not a romance, and his friendship did not insure her stepping into star roles when she signed with M-G-M.)

Ann was beautiful in *Easter Parade*. The role of the dancing star in this musical extravaganza was the heavy, but Ann managed to make her character likable. But this was still the "other woman" role—typecasting that she could not escape from in her M-G-M career.

Her dancing with Fred Astaire was fluid and graceful. Ten years earlier, when they were both working at RKO, Ann had been considered to co-star with Astaire in *A Damsel in Distress*, but the role went to Joan Fontaine.

"Shaking the Blues Away," which Berlin had written for *Ziegfeld Follies of 1927*, was Ann's tap solo in the musical. On a huge stage filled with flowing curtains, the camerawork embraced Ann's staccato taps. "The Girl on the Magazine Cover" showed Ann in a much different style, backed by chorus boys and using tremendous fans in a graceful and lovely production number.

Ann had finally appeared in an important "A" picture, and the critics expressed their enthusiastic approval of her work with such statements as: "Ann Miller suddenly blossoms forth as a beauty as well as a skillful tap dancer. The color photography does well by her. *Easter Parade* should set Ann Miller up on top"; and: "Ann Miller achieves the feat of being a seductive tap dancer, hitherto a contradiction in terms."

In 1949 never was a Hollywood film shot anywhere but on the studio soundstages. Co-directors Gene Kelly and Stanley Donen persuaded the M-G-M bosses for the very first time to go on location shooting in New York City which would enhance the film version of the 1944 Broadway hit *On the Town*.

True, not all of the film was shot in New York, but most of the exterior shots with the six stars—Kelly, Frank Sinatra, Jules Munshin, Betty Garrett, Ann Miller, and Vera-Ellen—did give the atmospheric flavor of three sailors on leave: the Brooklyn Navy Yard, the RCA building, Central Park, Little Italy, the Empire State building, Greenwich Village, and the roof of the Loew's building. In the M-G-M team tradition, Kelly and Sinatra had previously co-starred in *Anchors Aweigh* and *Take Me Out to the Ball Game*. Alice Pearce recreated her original stage role of "Lucy Schmeeler" for the movie.

Producer Arthur Freed did not like Leonard Bernstein's score for *On the Town*, which was considered avant-garde at the time, and consequently very little remained in the film version. One of the new numbers, "Prehistoric Man," served as a tap number for Ann, with Kelly, Sinatra, Munshin, and Betty Garrett in chorus backing her up.

The art department had to make a life-size sculpture, in the image of Munshin, of a *Pithecanthropus erectis*—the specimen Ann is studying at the museum and the pretext for the "Prehistoric Man" number. The art department also created a dinosaur skeleton, to be wrecked by Munshin, which consisted of 283 bones and was fifteen feet high and thirty-eight feet long.

On the Town, though a departure from the average musical motion picture, proved to be a very popular box-office attraction.

Ann's next work under her new contract was in a dance sequence which was hastily added to *The Kissing Bandit*. Both Frank Sinatra and Kathryn Grayson have said many times that *The Kissing Bandit*

The M-G-M look!

With Bob Hope at a charity event.

was the worst picture ever made. When a public preview was held, the studio brass agreed with the audience comment cards and the picture's release was postponed.

Sinatra and Grayson had previously been teamed well in *It Happened in Brooklyn* and *Anchors Aweigh*, but *The Kissing Bandit* was heavy-handed and tedious. In an attempt to inject life into the film's proceedings, Robert Alton choreographed the "Dance of Fury" for Ricardo Montalban, Cyd Charisse, and Ann. The trio was superb, and one wishes there could have been more of them. *The Kissing Bandit* remained dull and hokey, though the "Dance of Fury" did break the monotony. Sono Osato, fresh from her Broadway triumph in *On the Town*, was completely misused as a tavern dancer. Osato's original role of "Miss Turnstiles" in *On the Town* was played by Vera-Ellen in M-G-M's hit film musical.

Ann's next film, which she did not want to do, was a mistake. *Watch the Birdie*, photographed in black-and-white, was merely a witless excuse to utilize the comedy talent of Red Skelton in no less than three roles. (M-G-M always thought more was better.) Ann was wasted in a non-dancing comedy role as a beauty-contest winner, but she adored working with Red.

Skelton had made his screen debut in RKO's *Having Wonderful*

Time when Ann was under contract to that studio. They originally met on the vaudeville circuit and would subsequently do three movies together at M-G-M. Although Ann didn't dance in *Watch the Birdie*, she rehearsed in her free time when she wasn't before the cameras and, according to a publicity release, taught Skelton a new rhumba step between takes.

Their next film together, *Texas Carnival*, more than made up for *Watch the Birdie*. Ann played Texas dynamo "Sunshine Jackson," and her energetic characterization and dynamic dancing enlivened the movie considerably.

Choreographer Hermes Pan, who had served as dance director for most of Ann's films since her RKO days in *Stage Door* and *Radio City Revels*, devised a very elaborate square dance for the "Deep in the Heart of Texas" number entitled "The Flying Horse Music" by David Rose. Both star and dance director worked to make the dance steps novel. Ann's solo tap number, "It's Dynamite," had her tapping a glissando on a xylophone and roping and shooting off guns at Skelton. The Red Norvo Trio supplied the music.

A prerequisite for a movie with Esther Williams in it was that it have a swimming sequence. Esther was not cast as a swimming star in *Texas Carnival*, so the director, Charles Walters, devised a dream sequence, and for her routine an entire room was built on the bottom of the outdoor water tank which was used for all of Esther's swimming scenes.

In 1951 Howard Hughes then borrowed Ann's services for a role in his production of *Two Tickets to Broadway* at RKO, the studio he now owned. The movie, co-starring Gloria De Haven, Ann, and Barbara Lawrence as an act managed by bumbling Eddie Bracken, turned out to be a fairly routine, old-fashioned musical. The title is a bit misleading, for the act ends up on a Bob Crosby television show and not in a Broadway musical. Tony Martin and Janet Leigh also starred, and the famous vaudeville team Smith and Dale supplied ethnic humor as the patrons of the show business venture.

Ann danced "Let the Worry Bird Worry for You" in a Central Park setting, aided by Janet, Gloria, and Barbara. When *Two Tickets to Broadway* shows on TV, this number is deleted from the television prints. One wonders why since some of the other numbers in the film which are fairly awful are left intact. "It Began in Yucatan" was supposed to have been Ann's big solo number, but when she fell on the set's high Pyramid steps and hurt her back the number had to be cut. The music on the background soundtrack remains.

Back at M-G-M, Ann was again teamed with Skelton in a remake of *Roberta* entitled *Lovely to Look At*. She was typecast as showgirl "Bubbles Cassidy." Hermes Pan choreographed "I'll Be Hard to Handle" for Ann and a chorus of male dancers wearing wolf masks. The Champions, Marge and Gower, also danced in the picture, and Kathryn Grayson and Howard Keel sang the classic Jerome Kern songs. For the title song, Keel, reflected in four mirrors, sang four-part harmony with himself.

Designer Adrian devised a finale fashion show for the film which the critics variously felt was either elaborately dull or stunningly head-turning. The male members of the ballet portrayed "walking candelabras" and wore insulated underwear, through which wiring was run to gold circlets on their heads which held five electrically illuminated candles.

Next, in *Small Town Girl*, came the Busby Berkeley number that created a sensation. An extravagant production number, "I've Gotta Hear That Beat," had Ann tapping on a stage from which one hundred musical instruments and the hands playing them protruded. The effect was breathtaking. The *New York Times* reviewer wrote that Ann was "perfectly cast as a peppery Rialto gold-digger." Her other number was "My Gaucho," a firey flamenco dance without taps.

Bobby Van, as a Broadway hopeful, did a novelty number, "Hippity Hop," which consisted only of 8,523 hops done on both feet, bunny style. It was dull in 1953 and remained so when it was inserted into *That's Entertainment, Part 2*, twenty-three years later.

Ann Miller's motion picture career reached its peak in 1953, when she was cast as "Lois Lane" in *Kiss Me Kate*, starring with Kathryn Grayson and Howard Keel. It was the best movie she had done and she never looked more beautiful. The 3-D craze had swept Hollywood and M-G-M decided to film the hit musical in the three-dimensional process, although it was also released flat. The movie did not need the 3-D effects.

Ann's partner was played by Tommy Rall, a brilliant dancer making his screen debut after being featured in such Broadway shows as *Look Ma, I'm Dancin'*; *Small Wonder*; *Miss Liberty*; and *Call Me Madam*. Rall also appeared in Gene Kelly's ballet movie *Invitation to the Dance*. Ann and Rall did a superb rooftop duet to "Why Can't You Behave?"— with Rall doing breathtaking spins and leaps—and "Always True to You —in My Fashion." They were joined by Bobby Van and Bob Fosse for a show-stopping rendition of "Tom, Dick and Harry." The quartet, assisted by Carol Haney and Jeanne Coyne, exploded on the screen with "From This Moment On." What a treat it was to see a smooth jazz duet by Fosse and Carol Haney, who was Hermes Pan's assistant dance director.

At the beginning of the movie Ann bursts on the scene and makes the movie her own with "Too Darn Hot," possibly her best tap number to appear on film. Her use of a fan in close-ups showed off Ann's beauty to its best advantage. Even with the lyrics toned down for the movie and more beads added to her leotard, "Too Darn Hot" was a sizzling, sexy dance number. With *Kiss Me Kate*, Ann Miller finally starred in a class "A" motion picture.

She registered so outstandingly in *Kiss Me Kate* that M-G-M decided to send her on a three week publicity tour with the film. Ann was not allowed to do any dancing in these personal appearances. The studio also insured her legs for $1,000,000. At this time, producer Joe Pasternak was negotiating for the screen rights to *The Life of Eva Peron* to be called *Woman with a Whip*. Ann was the top candidate to

Ann and her mother, Clara Miller.

Her best role at Metro was in *Kiss Me Kate* and Ann was hot in "Too Darn Hot."

star as the first lady of Argentina, who had started out as a dancer. But nothing came of this, nor of reports that she was to star with Esther Williams in *Athena.*

Although her performance in *Kiss Me Kate* convinced the new studio boss, Dore Schary, to sign her to a new contract, M-G-M did not follow up this success with an Eleanor Powell–type assignment for Ann. Television was beginning to erode the motion picture business, and the studios faced severe economic problems. Ann was asked to take a cut in salary when she re-signed. She was aware of the difficulties and said: "Any star who's lucky enough to have a studio contract should give thanks. This is no time to act up. Everybody in our business should pull together."

Christmas of 1954 found her as a guest star, among many guest stars, in *Deep in My Heart*, a fictionalized film biography of composer Sigmund Romberg. The movie, starring Jose Ferrer and Helen Traubel, the Wagnerian soprano making her screen debut, was opulent, over-produced, and very long; all of M-G-M's twenty-eight soundstages were used in filming. Each of the production numbers was done in a way that usually ended ordinary musicals; hence, *Deep in My Heart* contained *nineteen* finales. Ann, costumed in an orange satin dress with twenty-three thousand beads, sang and danced "It" as a 1920's flapper from a revue entitled *Artists and Models*. The number was staged against a giant mural backdrop drawn by John Held, Jr., the famous cartoonist-chronicler of the twenties era.

The last movie in which Ann tap danced was *Hit the Deck*. The finale number, "Hallelujah!," was done on a reproduction of the fore main deck of a U.S. battleship, a set which covered an area of twenty-three thousand square feet. Ann was backed by what seemed a whole battalion of dancing sailors.

Another number was needed for Ann, since she was still playing the role of a nightclub dancer. Harold Hastings, who was then conducting the Broadway musical *The Pajama Game*, found an unpublished Vincent Youmans song and played it over the telephone for M-G-M conductor Johnny Green. The result, with new lyrics, was "Lady from the Bayou," which Ann did bare-footed. One reviewer wrote that he liked this routine by Ann because it "revealed a new and interesting personality in a dance that was something different."

Ann loved going on publicity trips for the studio, and in 1955 she became an ambassador for M-G-M. She was the first movie star ever to appear in person in Australia. The trip was in conjunction with *Hit the Deck* and she received huge ovations down under from the Aussies. She was also on hand for the opening of M-G-M's *Interrupted Melody*, the film biography of Australian opera star Marjorie Lawrence.

Traveling to other countries like Germany, Italy, Spain, France, England, Turkey, Egypt, Lebanon, and Jordan proved to be both exciting and educational for Ann and helped M-G-M.

"If I didn't sell these pictures for M-G-M I couldn't have taken my mother to Europe," Ann said. "All her life she has wanted to see Rome, Paris, and London. Now she is being treated to the trip because of all the work I'm doing."

A picture entitled *International Revue*, to be filmed in countries throughout the world, never materialized.

Ann also attended the opening of Hilton Hotels in Egypt and Rome, among others. Conrad Hilton, an ex-husband of Zsa Zsa Gabor, frequently dated Ann and she was his favorite dancing partner. But she also dated actors Dan Dailey and Philip Reed, Charles Isaacs (Eva Gabor's ex-husband), and Edmund Granger, who did *The Sands of Iwo Jima*, along with William V. O'Connor, the Assistant Attorney General for the state of California, and future husbands, oil men William Moss and Arthur Cameron of Texas.

A movie which was tailor-made for Ann's talent was *Silk Stockings*, but the role of the movie star went to Janis Paige. Ann, hurt by this slight, asked for her release from the studio; the request was denied.

Ann played straight comedy-dramatic roles in her last two M-G-M movies. In *The Opposite Sex*, which was based on *The Women*, Jack Cummings gave Ann a straight dramatic role and the musical chores were handled by June Allyson and Joan Collins, who had limited musical talent. June and Harry James repeated "Young Man with a Horn," which they had done previously in a film called *Two Girls and a Sailor*.

The Women was a stinging, biting, brilliant movie about divorce.

It had a distinguished cast consisting of Norma Shearer, Joan Crawford, Rosalind Russell, Paulette Goddard, Joan Fontaine, Ruth Hussey, Mary Boland, and Marjorie Main. The musical remake fared better than most re-done properties, primarily because of Ann Miller, Ann Sheridan, and Dolores Gray, who was particularly effective in Rosalind Russell's original role. Ann's role of "Gloria," originally played by Paulette Goddard in *The Women*, had her saying the now-famous line "Where I spit, no grass grows!"

The stars were dressed beautifully by designer Helen Rose, who created more than 250 costumes for them. The beauty parlor set, which appeared on-screen for approximately eight minutes, was designed, built, and decorated over a six-week period by thirty-eight people, at a cost of more than twenty-five thousand dollars.

Ann and Dolores had a staged free-for-all in this movie, reminiscent of the fight between Ann and Penny Singleton in *Go West, Young Lady*. M-G-M supplied a professional boxer to demonstrate fast uppercuts and body blows to the two stars for their battle. Ann and Dolores, however, have remained great friends through the years.

William Green sees Ann off on a studio trip.

After she had appeared in so many "B" movies, it is sad that Ann's last M-G-M film was in that category. *The Great American Pastime* was a harmless little comedy about little-league baseball which ended up in theatrical release as the second feature. Ann was still the "other woman." For the little-league teams the movie used forty-five youngsters ranging in age from nine to twelve, thirteen of whom had to be southpaws. Duke Snider, Roy Campanella, Pee Wee Reese, and Sandy Amoros of the Brooklyn Dodgers all okayed the use of their names in the script. Anne Francis' dog even got a part in this movie. Sadly, Ann asked for her release and left M-G-M in 1958.

After Louis B. Mayer died and Dore Schary became M-G-M's chief, Hollywood began to fall like Rome. Fifteen years after Ann left M-G-M, and for the fiftieth anniversary of Metro-Goldwyn-Mayer, Jack Haley, Jr., dug into the vaults and put together a tribute to the studio which had been responsible for so many glittering movie musicals. *That's Entertainment!* (1974) consisted of film clips of some of the great moments from M-G-M musicals and featured some of the stars taking a nostalgic tour through the then crumbling studio sets and buildings.

But the musical numbers were the important thing, and Haley presented them with great care. "I've Gotta Hear That Beat," Ann's number from *Small Town Girl*, and "Hallelujah!," from *Hit the Deck*, were included. And again Ann went on tour to promote the film, just as she had done years before, to Australia, London, Spain, France, Puerto Rico, and Hawaii.

Two years later, in 1976, Gene Kelly and Fred Astaire co-hosted *That's Entertainment, Part 2*, which presented not only more musical numbers but clips from M-G-M's comedies and dramas. The result was not satisfying. The new sequences looked like a television special, and the movie was more a scrapbook of Kelly's and Astaire's work than a tribute to M-G-M. However, Ann's number "From This Moment On," from *Kiss Me Kate*, stood out as one of the few high spots in the film. M-G-M sent her to Vienna for the Salsburg Film Festival again to promote the movie and to act as their good will ambassador.

Ann is wild about animals and in 1976, Paramount persuaded her to appear in a "cameo" role in *Won Ton Ton, the Dog Who Saved Hollywood*. The movie was a dog too and disappeared quickly. Somehow the producers had persuaded seventy-five other stars to also lend their presence to this movie, but the bits were mercifully short, and it was difficult to spot or even recognize most of the performers. After the movie was released Ann said: "Hollywood's going to the DOGS!"

Never again will there be a great studio like Metro-Goldwyn-Mayer nor the kinds of films that were made during the Golden Age of Hollywood. But television and revival movie-houses bring them back to us and we can still see Ann and her M-G-M family doing what they did best. But on the horizon looms numerous television appearances and belated Broadway stardom for Ann, giving a new dimension to her many faceted career.

Release date: July 8, 1948

CAST

Hannah Brown	JUDY GARLAND
Don Hewes	FRED ASTAIRE
Jonathan Harrow III	Peter LAWFORD
Nadine Hale	Ann MILLER
Francois	Jules Munshin
Mike the bartender	Clinton Sundberg
Essie	Jeni LeGon
Singer	Richard Beavers
Al, stage manager for Ziegfeld	Dick Simmons
Boy in "Drum Crazy"	Jimmy Bates
Cabbie	Jimmy Dodd

Cop who gives Johnny a ticket	Robert Emmett O'Connor
Specialty dancers	Patricia Jackson, Bobbie Priest, Dee Turnell
Hat models	Lola Albright, Joi Lansing
"Delineator" twins	Lynn and Jean Romer
Modiste	Helen Heigh
Marty	Wilson Wood
Dog act	Hector and His Pals—Carmi Tryon
Sam, the valet	Peter Chong
Drug clerk	Nolan Leary
Mary	Doris Kemper
Headwaiter	Frank Mayo
Bar patron	Benay Venuta

CREDITS

Director: Charles Walters *Producer*: Arthur Freed *Screenplay*: Sidney Sheldon, Frances Goodrich, Albert Hackett *Based on a story by*: Frances Goodrich, Albert Hackett *Music and lyrics*: Irving Berlin *Director of photography*: Harry Stradling, A.S.C. *Dance direction*: Robert Alton *Musical conductors*: Johnny Green, Georgie Stoll *Orchestrations*: Conrad Salinger, Van Cleave, Leo Arnaud *Art directors*: Cedric Gibbons, Jack Martin Smith *Film editor*: Albert Akst *Running time*: 103 minutes.

SONGS

"Happy Easter," "Easter Parade," "Drum Crazy," "It Only Happens When I Dance with You," "Everybody's Doing It Now," "I Want to Go Back to Michigan," "A Fella with an Umbrella," "I Love a Piano," "Snooky Ookums," "Ragtime Violin," "When the Midnight Choo Choo Leaves for Alabam'," "Shaking the Blues Away," "Stepping Out with My Baby," "A Couple of Swells," "Better Luck Next Time," "Beautiful Faces Need Beautiful Clothes," "The Girl on the Magazine Cover."

SYNOPSIS

Don Hewes (Fred Astaire) arrives at the apartment of his partner, Nadine Hale (Ann Miller) with Easter presents for her. Jonathan Harrow III (Peter Lawford) also arrives with a Pug puppy for Nadine and to give his friends a going away dinner celebration. However, Nadine tells them both that she won't be leaving for Chicago to start a new engagement because she has signed to star in a new Broadway edition of the *Ziegfeld Follies*.

Hewes is angry with Nadine and vows that he can make a dance partner out of any one of the chorus girls at the club he goes to for a drink with Harrow. He offers a dancing job to Hannah Brown (Judy Garland).

Rehearsals the next day, Easter Sunday, show that Hannah is not much of a dancer. But after rehearsals, walking down Fifth Avenue in the Easter parade, and seeing Nadine regally walking her dogs, Hewes vows that in one year's time Hannah will be getting the attention at the Easter parade.

The new act, "Juanita and Hewes," is a disaster. When Nadine next sees Hewes, she tells him Hannah must stop imitating her. Hewes realizes that is what's wrong with the act. Now, as "Hannah and Hewes," they have a smash act and are invited to audition for Mr. Ziegfeld for his *Follies of 1912*, the show in which Nadine is starring.

Hewes turns down the *Follies*; he says he doesn't want to share the marquee with Nadine. When the show opens, Nadine is superb, the *Follies* a smash. But Hewes has good news. It seems that theatrical producer Dillingham wants the act for his new show which will open in New York the day before Easter. Meanwhile, Harrow has fallen in love with Hannah, not knowing she is Hewes's partner. But Hannah is in love with Hewes.

The Easter Parade.

After their smashing opening night, Hannah and Hewes go to the Ziegfeld Room, where Nadine is appearing, to celebrate. Nadine has been told by her maid Essie (Jeni LeGon) that the show wasn't good, and after Nadine's number she persuades Hewes to dance with her again. Hurt, Hannah leaves.

Hewes is waiting for Hannah when she finally comes home, but she won't believe that Hewes doesn't really want Nadine back. Hewes tries in vain to convince her that he really loves her.

The next morning, Harrow arrives at Hannah's apartment. He finally does convince her to go to Hewes. Harrow then calls Nadine to say that he will escort her in the Easter parade.

Easter presents from Hannah arrive at Hewes's apartment. The two make up and keep their date for the Easter parade.

CRITICAL REACTION

The *Hollywood Reporter:*

"*Easter Parade* is an entertainment package as spectacular as an Easter bonnet, as full of fun as searching for an Easter egg, and about as capricious, gay, and giddy as an Easter bunny. Which is to say it is a wonderful show—sparkling, tuneful, bright. An artist with the charm of Fred Astaire has no right to take it easy . . . *Easter Parade* shows him at his very best. [Judy Garland] sings and performs with irresis-

With Fred Astaire: "It Only Happens When I Dance with You."

"Shaking the Blues Away"

tible Garland charm. Ann Miller, the next star on the *Easter Parade* agenda, takes a supporting role, dances a magnificent tap solo in addition to a couple of appearances with Astaire, reads a few lines and does herself more good than she has in years. She looks beautiful, her wardrobe is terrific, and since there has never been any argument about the quality of her hoofing, it is a certainty that she is now in the big leagues."

Daily Variety:
"Here is a Technicolor musical in the grand style . . . big and joyous and altogether heartwarming. Picture firmly establishes Judy Garland as the screen's first lady of terps and tunes. There are some exceptionally bright contributions by Fred Astaire, Ann Miller, Peter Lawford and Jules Munshin. Miss Miller shines in 'Shaking the Blues Away.' This is a bright star in producer Arthur Freed's crown."

Thomas M. Pryor in the *New York Times*:
"With several Irving Berlin songs to record and with Fred Astaire, Judy Garland and Ann Miller itching to exercise their accomplished legs and adequate vocal cords, it's no wonder that

the slim story line on which *Easter Parade* is spun is almost completely lost in the shuffle. But don't give that loss a second thought. In solo and in tandem with either Miss Garland or Miss Miller the incomparable Astaire glides effortlessly through numerous routines. Although Judy Garland gets the top billing, she also gets stiff competition from the long-legged Ann Miller, who does an especially graceful ballroom dance with the master. Somehow we feel that Miss Miller pairs better with Astaire."

Howard Barnes in the *New York Herald Tribune*:
"*Easter Parade* employs a bundle of the celebrated composer's songs. Charles Walters has made *Easter Parade* a disarming and delightful charade. The musical comedy interludes of thirty-odd years ago are more lavish than they may have been at the old New Amsterdam Theater, but they are generally captivating. Peter Lawford and Ann Miller are on hand to contribute romantic angles and song and dance fillup to the proceeding. *Easter Parade* is a bit thin on plot, but it has music and dancing to delight the most captious screengoer."

Release date: December 30, 1949

CAST

Gabey . . . . GENE KELLY
Chip . . . . FRANK SINATRA
Brunhilde Esterhazy . . . . BETTY GARRETT
Claire Huddesen . . . . ANN MILLER
Ozzie . . . . Jules MUNSHIN
Ivy Smith . . . . Vera-ELLEN
Madame Dilyouska . . . . Florence Bates
Lucy Schmeeler . . . . Alice Pearce
Professor . . . . George Meader
Working girl . . . . Bea Benedaret
Headwaiter . . . . Hans Conried
Dancer in green . . . . Carol Haney

Betty Garrett, Frank Sinatra, Ann, Jules Munshin,
Vera-Ellen and Gene Kelly.

CREDITS

Directors: Gene Kelly, Stanley Donen *Producer:* Arthur Freed *Screenplay:* Adolph Green, Betty Comden *Based on the musical play:* book by Adolph Green, Betty Comden, from an idea by Jerome Robbins, music by Leonard Bernstein, lyrics by Adolph Green, Betty Comden, Leonard Bernstein *Directed on the stage by* George Abbott *produced by* Oliver Smith, Paul Feigay *Director of photography:* Harold Rosson, A.S.C. *Associate producer:* Roger Edens *Art directors:* Cedric Gibbons, Jack Martin Smith *Set decorators:* Edwin B. Willis, Jack D. Moore *Music supervisor and conductor:* Lennie Hayton *Orchestral arrangements:* Conrad Salinger, Robert Franklyn, Wally Heglin *Vocal arrangements:* Saul Chaplin *Incidental score:* Roger Edens, Saul Chaplin, Conrad Salinger *Costumes:* Helen Rose *Makeup:* Jack Dawn *Hairstyles:* Sydney Guilaroff *Special effects:* Warren Newcombe *Sound recorder:* John A. Williams *Assistant director:* Jack Gertsman *Production manager:* Hugh Boswell *Color consultants:* Henri Jaffa, James Gooch *Film editor:* Ralph E. Winters *Running time:* 98 minutes.

SONGS

Music and lyrics: Leonard Bernstein, Adolph Green, Betty Comden, Roger Edens. "Miss Turnstiles Ballet: A Day in New York," "I Feel Like I'm Not Out of Bed Yet," "New York, New York," "Come Up to My Place," "You're Awful," "On the Town," "Count on Me," "Main Street," "Prehistoric Man."

SYNOPSIS

Three sailors, Gabey (Gene Kelly), Chip (Frank Sinatra) and Ozzie (Jules Munshin) are on their first twenty-four-hour pass in New York City. Chip suggests that they pick up dates and see the sights.

In the subway, a poster of Ivy Smith (Vera-Ellen), "Miss Turnstiles" for the month of June, is being put up. Gabey likes what he sees and takes the picture. At the next station Ivy is being photographed and Gabey is asked to pose with her. She then disappears into the crowd. The sailors hail a cab, driven by Brunhilde Esterhazy (Betty Garrett), to drive them to the next station. But at Columbus Circle they miss Ivy. The cab is due back in the garage, but Hildy has fallen for Chip and agrees to help them search for Ivy.

Their first stop is the Museum of Anthropological History. Claire Huddesen (Ann Miller) is doing research on prehistoric man and Ozzie is a dead ringer for the statue. By accident, a huge dinosaur is wrecked and they flee the museum. Hildy suggests they split up and look separately for Ivy. The two couples promise to meet Gabey at 8:30 that night at the top of the Empire State Building.

Hildy's roommate, Lucy Schmeeler (Alice Pearce), is home with a cold and ruins Hildy's plans to be alone with Chip.

Gabey goes alone to Symphonic Hall. Ivy is taking a dance class from Madame Dilyouska (Florence Bates) but works as a cooch dancer at Coney Island to pay for her lessons. When Gabey finds Ivy, she promises to meet him at 8:30.

When she arrives at the Empire State Building, Claire and Hildy decide not to spoil

Ann measures the head of her "Pithecanthropus erectis," Jules Munshin.

Gabey's impression that she is a big celebrity. The couples go on the town. Claire bribes nightclub headwaiter François (Hans Conried) to make a fuss over "Miss Turnstiles." But Ivy leaves the party at 11:30. Hildy gets Lucy to join them as Gabey's date. When Gabey takes Lucy home, he apologizes for being downcast and says that he is not the right man for her.

Later, at a bar, they see Madame Dilyouska, who tells Gabey the truth about Ivy and where she is working. The group heads for Brooklyn in Hildy's cab, with the police following closely behind.

They find the show where Ivy is working. She confesses her deception to Gabey and they discover that they are from the same hometown, Meadowville, Indiana.

The police finally catch up with them. The boys, in drag, and Claire and Hildy, in harem outfits, try to blend into the show that's in progress. Gabey, Chip, and Ozzie escape right into a waiting shore-patrol wagon. The girls plead for their guys and manage to talk the police out of pressing charges. Ivy, Hildy, and Claire get a police escort to the Brooklyn Navy Yard. They get to the ship just before 6:00 a.m. and are able to say goodbye to the three sailors.

"Prehistoric Man"

CRITICAL REACTION

The *Hollywood Reporter:*

"*On the Town* is a motion picture done in the style of a smart Broadway review . . . its almost total absence of story emphasizes the song and dance specialties throughout. The numbers fairly zip along. The headliners form their own ensemble background as one by one each steps out for his particular specialty. Gene Kelly's dancing sparks the proceedings with every routine, and Frank Sinatra's voice and harassed manner makes his role a delight. Betty Garrett's clowning pleases, and Ann Miller's warbling and hoofing are tops."

Bosley Crowther in the *New York Times:*

"Metro's crackling screen version of the musical *On the Town*—gaiety, rhythm, numbers and a good wholesome dash of light romance —have been artfully blended together in this bright Technicolor comedy. The over-all picture flits and frolics with the same carefree delight as did the popular original—and with equal originality, too. 'Prehistoric Man' is a new item which has been neatly contrived for

Ann Miller and giggly Jules Munshin, who comprise the third duo. Six very spirited young people have great fun from *On the Town*. And so do we."

Otis L. Guernsey, Jr., in the *New York Herald Tribune:*

"Under the direction of Gene Kelly and Stanley Donen, the cast gives a slam-bang rendition of a book, music, lyrics and dances that are not always as good as they seem. But it is the sort of show which is not to be denied and which is put over by sheer force of unfailing gaiety. One suspects that it was Kelly, working both before and behind the camera, who gave *On the Town* its get-up-and-go. Munshin, linked with Ann Miller, handles most of the antic humor, including a wild parody of a native dance performance in a museum. Against a lot of authentic backgrounds *On the Town* has recorded enough gyrating, fast-paced, open-handed musical nonsense to last even a sailor a month. New York certainly looks like a wonderful town while it is around and the Music Hall a wonderful place to be entertained."

Alice Pearce, Frank Sinatra, Betty Garrett, Gene Kelly, Ann, Jules Munshin: "Count on Me."

The 24-hour shore leave is over and the girls say goodbye to their guys.

Release date: January, 1949

CAST

Ricardo	FRANK SINATRA
Teresa	KATHRYN GRAYSON
Chico	J. Carrol NAISH
Isabella	Mildred NATWICK
Don José	Mikhail RASUMNY
General Torro	Billy GILBERT
Bianca	Sono OSATO
Colonel Gómez	Clinton Sundberg
Count Belmonte	Carleton Young
Juanita	Edna Skinner
Guitarist	Vincente Gomez

Pepito	Henry Mirelez
Pablo	Nick Thompson
Francisco	Jose Dominguez
Lotso	Albert Morin
Estebán	Pedro Regas
Postman	Julian Rivero
Fernando	Mitchell Lewis
Grandee	Byron Foulger

Dance specialties
RICARDO MONTALBAN, *ANN MILLER*, CYD CHARISSE

CREDITS

Director: Laslo Benedek *Producer:* Joe Pasternak *Original screenplay:* Isobel Lennart, John Briard Harding *Director of photography:* Robert Surtees *Music supervisor and conductor:* George Stoll *Musical arrangements:* Leo Arnaud *Incidental score:* George Stoll, Albert Sendry, Scott Bradley, Andre Previn *Additional orchestrations:* Albert Sendry, Calvin Jackson, Conrad Salinger, Robert Van Eps, Paul Marquardt, Earl Brent *Dance director:* Stanley Donen *Art directors:* Cedric Gibbons, Randall Duell *Set decorators:* Edwin B. Willis, Jack D. Moore *Costumes:* Walter Plunkett *Makeup:* Jack Dawn *Hair stylist:* Sydney Guilaroff *Special effects:* A. Arnold Gillespie *Sound recorder:* Wilhelm W. Brockway *Assistant director:* Marvin Stuart *Production manager:* Sergei Petschnikoff *Color consultant:* Henri Jaffe *Film editor:* Adrienne Fazan *Running time:* 100 minutes.

SONGS

Music and lyrics: Nacio Herb Brown, Edward Heyman, Earl Brent. "Dance of Fury," "What's Wrong With Me?," "If I Steal a Kiss," "Senorita," "Siesta," "Love Is Where You Find It," "Tomorrow Means Romance," "The Whip Dance."

SYNOPSIS

A letter from Boston arrives for Chico (J. Carrol Naish) from Ricardo (Frank Sinatra), the son of a bandit chief known as "The Kissing Bandit." The letter states that Ricardo has been studying to manage the business and Chico thinks he is coming to take over being a bandit, like his father.

When Ricardo arrives, Chico learns that he has been studying hotel management and is there to take over running the Inn, a sideline of his father's. Chico manages to convince him to try to follow in his father's footsteps.

Meanwhile, Teresa (Kathryn Grayson), the governor's daughter, is leaving school and is on the coach that the bandits choose for Ricardo's first hold-up. She is traveling with her aunt Isabella (Mildred Natwick). The horses run away with the stagecoach. When it finally comes to a stop, Ricardo doesn't kiss Teresa.

Teresa's father, Don José (Mikhail Rasumny) vows to catch the bandit and have him hanged. But Teresa gives a false description of Ricardo and wonders why she wasn't kissed. Ricardo rides to the Governor's *hacienda* to serenade Teresa. Chico rescues him from the Governor's men and tries to get him interested in Bianca (Sono Osato).

Count Belmonte (Carleton Young) and his aide General Torro (Billy Gilbert) arrive at the Inn. They have come from Spain to collect taxes. Belmonte and Torro are overpowered by the bandits and tied up. Colonel Gómez (Clinton Sundberg) arrives at the Inn looking for the kissing bandit and learns that Belmonte has arrived from Spain.

Ricardo and Chico masquerade as the Spaniards, thinking they will be able to steal the tax money. Don José, evading the question of taxes, gives them an impressive reception. At the fiesta, a trio (Ricardo Montalban, Ann Miller, and Cyd Charisse) entertain the guests by dancing the "Dance of Fury."

J. Carrol Naish, Clinton Sundberg, Frank Sinatra

Ricardo tells Teresa of his love for her. Chico interrupts—he has found nothing in the treasury. He also tells Ricardo that as a bandit he has no right to Teresa.

General Toro and Count Belmonte arrive at the party. Ricardo and Chico are arrested but manage to escape through the ineptitude of Gómez. Ricardo, seeing Teresa with Belmonte, goes to her aid and knocks out the count.

Don José hires Chico as his tax collector, much to Isabella's delight, and orders Belmonte and Torro out of California.

Ricardo is packing for his return to Boston when he hears Teresa serenading him. He finally kisses her.

CRITICAL REACTION

Daily Variety:

"Produced along travesty lines, *The Kissing Bandit* is pretty flimsy stuff, but occasionally blossoms forth with laughs and two crackerjack dancing numbers. Highlights are the whip dance as terped by Sono Osato, and 'Dance of Fury,' tripling stepping talents of Ricardo Montalban, Ann Miller and Cyd Charisse, both offerings accompanied by exciting music of Nacio Herb Brown. Song numbers are spotted frequently and melodically, too, but picture will need strongest kind of selling to hold up."

Otis L. Guernsey, Jr., in the
New York Herald Tribune:

"In M-G-M's *The Kissing Bandit*, Frank Sinatra wanders about in a grand Technicolored vacuum for about 100 minutes . . . falling somewhere between whimsy and burlesque. Sinatra is a fragile hero in search of some worthwhile comedy ideas. Even his song numbers are something less than satisfying in this film, leaving him absolutely nothing to fall back on. The rest of the cast fares no better in [this] limp Spanish omelette. Two dance sequences, one by Sono Osato, and one by a trio composed of Ricardo Montalban, Ann Miller and Cyd Charisse are the best footage in the show. Elsewhere *The Kissing Bandit* falls as flat as a bad joke with a big build-up."

Bosley Crowther in the *New York Times*:
"The script is as void of spark and luster as the decor and dancers are full. And although it is highly potential, so far as plot is concerned, it offers some bleak and barren burlesque for the ready and willing cast to perform. Except for appearing gawky, which seems not very hard for him to do, and singing his songs rather nicely [Sinatra] contributes little to the show. Also, it must be mentioned that Sono Osato comes through with a spirited Spanish number in the one opportunity she has. And Ann Miller, Ricardo Montalban and Cyd Charisse stomp and whip with thrilling grace through a thumping and thundering 'Dance of Fury,' which marks their one appearance—and the best spectacle—in the film. But the script isn't there and Laslo Benedek has done little as director with what he has. *The Kissing Bandit* quite significantly contains only one listless kiss."

Cyd Charisse, Ricardo Montalban, Ann.

Release date: January 12, 1951

CAST

Rusty Cameron, Pop Cameron,
   Grandpop Cameron . . . . RED SKELTON
Lucia Corlane . . . . ARLENE DAHL
Miss Lucky Vista . . . . ANN MILLER
Grantland D. Farns . . . . Leon AMES
Mrs. Shanway . . . . Pam BRITTON
Mr. Hugh Shanway . . . . Richard ROBER
Man who undresses . . . . Dick Wessel
Starlets . . . . Jacqueline Duval, Paula Drew, Georgia Pelham

CREDITS

Director: Jack Donohue *Producer*: Harry Ruskin *Screenplay*: Ivan Tors, Devery Freeman, Harry Ruskin, *Based on a story by*: Marshall Neilan, Jr., *Director of photography*: Paul C. Vogel, A.S.C. *Art directors*: Cedric Gibbons, Eddie Imazu *Music*: Georgie Stoll *Recording supervisor*: Douglas Shearer *Set decorators*: Edwin B. Willis, Keogh Gleason *Special effects*: A. Arnold Gillespie, Warren Newcombe *Hairstyles*: Sydney Guilaroff *Makeup*: William J. Tuttle *Film editor*: Robert Watts *Running time*: 71 minutes.

SYNOPSIS

Rusty Cameron (Red Skelton) nearly drowns when he is filming a boat launching. He has become a cameraman hoping to pay off debts on his family's photographic equipment shop. Rusty is saved by Lucia Corlane (Arlene Dahl), heiress to an uncompleted real estate project.

Lucia wants the project completed so that she can recover the capital she has invested in it. Her financial adviser, Grantland D. Farns (Leon Ames), unscrupulously bribes building inspector Hugh Shanway (Richard Rober) into giving an unfavorable report in order to force Lucia to sell the property at a loss. When Rusty films the opening ceremony at the project, he unknowingly records Farns and Shanway discussing their proposed bargain.

Rusty's father, Pop Cameron (Red Skelton), accidentally spoils the developing of the film, and Farns and Shanway evade detection when the pictures are shown to Lucia, Mrs. Shanway (Pam Britton) and Miss Lucky Vista (Ann Miller), a beauty-prize winner who helped publicize the opening.

When Rusty reassembles the film Lucia realizes there is a plot against her. Farns and Shanway are determined to get the evidence away from Rusty and use Miss Lucky Vista as a decoy to charm the negative from him. She fails but wins over Grandpop Cameron (Red Skelton) instead.

Farns and Shanway then trap Rusty and Lucia at the Corlane plant. They manage to escape in a two-story straddle truck, and, after a frenzied chase, Rusty and Lucia deposit the crooks in the hands of the police.

CRITICAL REACTION

The *Hollywood Reporter*:

"To make up for lack of plot [in *Watch the Birdie*] there are no less than three Red Skel-

With Red Skelton.

tons. Harry Ruskin has geared his production strictly for laughs [and] furnishes an optical treat by casting Arlene Dahl, Ann Miller and Pam Britton, three lovely lasses who take care of the pulchritude side most effectively and delightfully. Skelton handles the three generations with genuine artistry. Miss Dahl is beautiful and capable as the ingenue, and Miss Miller shows some real comedy talent as the beauty contest winner trying to vamp Red out of the film evidence."

Daily Variety:
"*Watch the Birdie* is a slap-happy comedy venture. The hokum dished out is played as broad as possible. Among the risibility-ticklers spotted through the footage, one of the best is the undressing scene between Skelton and Dick Wessel in a doctor's office. There's also fun to be found in Ann Miller's take-off on all of the 'Misses This and That' who endorse everything from hot dogs to grapefruit as an excuse for cheesecake art. In the gam display Miss Miller registers."

Bosley Crowther in the *New York Times*:
"Either Red Skelton is weakening or his writers have sadly let him down in M-G-M's *Watch the Birdie*. There is little credit in it

for the star nor are [his] conversations with himself of any particular help. Miss Dahl has the job of playing straight to a virtual vacuum, and Ann Miller bears up rather bravely in a small and humiliating role. Jack Donohue's direction is desperately anxious—but in vain. The time has come for Mr. Skelton to look for a new formula."

Otis L. Guernsey, Jr., in the *New York Herald Tribune*:
"Red Skelton's particular costume of humor is worn right down to the underweave in *Watch the Birdie* at the Capitol. In one of the weakest scripts on the record, the comedian is left to rely on his own devices as he muddles through a story of crime and photography. There is so little satire in this screenplay that the sight of two men trying to disrobe in a narrow space and getting in each other's way [is] dragged in by sheer force of necessity to give the cast something to do. Skelton has the added burden of contributing some of the support himself. Arlene Dahl and Ann Miller are the two girls in his life, and Leon Ames and Richard Rober are the villains in a last flurry of nonsense. You don't have to watch this birdie for very long before identifying it as the kind of birdie that one associates with Thanksgiving."

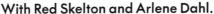

With Red Skelton and Arlene Dahl.

TEXAS CARNIVAL

Release date: October 5, 1951

CAST

Debbie Telford	ESTHER WILLIAMS
Cornie Quinell	RED SKELTON
Slim Shelby	HOWARD KEEL
Sunshine Jackson	Ann MILLER
Marilla Sabinas	Paula RAYMOND
Dan Sabinas	Keenan WYNN
Sheriff Jackson	Tom TULLY
Tex Hodgkins	Glenn Strange
Concessionaires	Dick Wessel, Donald McBride
Mrs. Gaytes	Marjorie Wood
Hotel clerk	Hans Conried

Mr. Gaytes	Thurston Hall
Juggler	Duke Johnson
Bellboy	Wilson Wood
Card player	Michael Dugan

And
FOY WILLING and ORCHESTRA, RED NORVO TRIO

CREDITS

Director: Charles Walters *Producer:* Jack Cummings *Screenplay:* Dorothy Kingsley *Story:* George Wells, Dorothy Kingsley *Musical director:* David Rose *Choreography:* Hermes Pan *Director of photography:* Robert Planck, A.S.C. *Technicolor consultants:* Henri Jaffa, James Gooch *Art directors:* Cedric Gibbons, William Ferrari *Recording supervisor:* Douglas Shearer *Set decorators:* Edwin B. Willis, Keogh Gleason *Special effects:* A. Arnold Gillespie, Warren Newcombe *Women's costume designer:* Helen Rose *Hairstyles:* Sydney Guilaroff *Makeup:* William Tuttle *Film editor:* Adrienne Fazan, A.C.E. *Running time:* 77 minutes.

SONGS

Music and lyrics: Harry Warren, Dorothy Fields, June Hersey, Don Swander, Maurice Vandair. "Whoa, Emma," "Young Folks Should Be Married," "Cornie's Pitch," "Schnaps," "It's Dynamite," "Deep in the Heart of Texas."

SYNOPSIS

Cornelius "Cornie" Quinell (Red Skelton), a barker for the Belrow Western Carnival, and his assistant, Debbie Telford (Esther Williams), are trouping through Texas. Debbie's job is to sit on a breakaway seat over a tank of water. If a customer hits the target with a ball, she drops into the water. Debbie is disgusted with her "career" and plans to go back home to Montana.

Cattle baron Dan Sabinas (Keenan Wynn), while drunk, is being cheated by two carnival men. When Cornie saves him, Sabinas insists on giving him his Cadillac, but Cornie refuses. However, he and Debbie are forced to flee from the wrath of the two carnival men and escape in Sabinas's car. They drive to Sa-

With Esther Williams and Red Skelton.

"It's Dynamite"

binas's hotel with the intention of returning the car.

At the hotel Cornie and Debbie are mistaken for Sabinas and his sister, Marilla. In the meantime Marilla (Paula Raymond) has traced Sabinas to Mexico. Informed about the impostors, she orders Slim Shelby (Howard Keel), the Sabinas ranch foreman, to keep an eye on Cornie and Debbie. Naturally, Shelby falls for Debbie. Cornie also becomes desirable to Sunshine Jackson (Ann Miller), oil millionairess and daughter of the local sheriff (Tom Tully).

In a poker game, Cornie ends up owing Tex Hodgkins (Glenn Strange), a tough cattleman, seventeen thousand dollars. Hodgkins makes him a sporting proposition—each man will enter the chuckwagon race with each driving his own wagon and the winner taking all. Cornie, hanging on for dear life, wins the race!

Sabinas and Marilla show up and expose Cornie and Debbie, who head back to the carnival. But Shelby and Sunshine trail them there for a happy reunion.

CRITICAL REACTION

The *Hollywood Reporter:*
"*Texas Carnival* is a bright, energetic comedy with music. The story is generally effective in the affectionate satirical shafts it aims at Texas. If the situations are stereotyped, the dialogue is glib, frequently funny. Ann Miller whams home a portrait of a vivacious Texas extrovert with vigorous skill. Her dynamic dance number, "It's Dynamite," is excellently done, staged with great vigor by Hermes Pan."

Bosley Crowther in the *New York Times:*
"Despite the generous presence of Esther Williams, Ann Miller, Howard Keel and Keenan Wynn, all ready and able, in the cast of *Texas Carnival*, this new Metro musical at Loew's State is entirely Red Skelton's show. For those who like Mr. Skelton, this probably will be all to the good. However, with others in the picture who also may have their fans, the lesser part of politeness might have been to let them do more. We might have been happy with a

good bit more of Mr. Wynn, for he is rich as the roaring Texas Gotrocks in the few scenes that he plays. And likewise the twinkling Miss Miller may not be a great dramatic star, but her dancing is highly stimulating in the one fast number that she has. But then it may be that all of them did have more to do and their stuff later was cut from the picture. Somehow it looks that way."

Joe Pihodna in the
New York Herald Tribune:
"A funny and fast-moving Technicolor movie. Esther Williams and Red Skelton form an engaging team in a nonsensical film which has something to do with a Texas oil millionaire and a carnival. Ann Miller, an energetic dancer, works so hard that a viewer is apt to sweat just watching her. By the way, *Texas Carnival* pokes gentle fun at Texans, who, being big and strong, are probably able to take it."

With Tom Tully and Red Skelton.

"Deep in the Heart of Texas"

Release date: November, 1951

CAST

Dan Carter	TONY MARTIN
Nancy Peterson	JANET LEIGH
Hannah Holbrook	GLORIA DE HAVEN
Lew Conway	EDDIE BRACKEN
Joyce Campbell	ANN MILLER
S. F. Rogers	Barbara LAWRENCE
Himself	Bob CROSBY
Acrobatic specialty	The CHARLIVELS
Harry	Joe Smith
Leo	Charles Dale
Willard Glendon	Taylor Holmes
Sailor	Buddy Baer

Wardrobe woman	Frieda Stoll
Bus driver	Fred L. Gillett
Mr. Peterson	Norval Mitchell
Mrs. Peterson	Helen Spring
McGiven	John Gallaudet
Housekeeper	Isabel Randolph
Bus terminal guard	Donald MacBride
Desk clerk	John Sheehan
Porter	Don Blackman

BITS

Chorus girl Vera Miles *Redhead* Joy Lansing *Bit showgirls* Mara Corday, Joan Evans *Bit man* George Nader *Brunette* Linda Williams *Blonde* Ann Zika *Maid* Libby Taylor *Doorman* Herman Cantor *Receptionist* Millicent Deming *Agent* Jerry Hausner *Bit dispatcher* Jack Gargan *1st girl* Jane Easton *2nd girl* Shirley Tegge *3rd girl* Martha O'Brian *4th girl* Lucy Knoch *5th girl* Rosalee Calvert *6th girl* Joan Shawlee *7th girl* Joan Barton *8th girl* Shirley Whitney *9th girl* Marilyn Johnson *Pretty girl* Gwen Caldwell *1st girl* Barbara Freking *2nd girl* Mona Knox *3rd girl* Rosemary Knighton *4th girl* Marie Thomas *Chorus girls* Jean Corbett, Helen Hayden, Claudette Thornton, Hazel Shaw, Barbara Logan, Charlotte Alpert, Victoria Lynn, Jeane Dyer, Pat Hall, Maura Donatt *Bit midget* Billy Curtis *Men with Tuxes* Mike Lally, Bennett Green *Bit waiter* Larry Barton *Usher* Gene Banks *Bit cheerleader* Vincent Graeff *Showgirls* June McCall, Joan Olander, Noreen Mortensen, Joel Robinson, Georgia Clancy, Elizabeth Burgess, Barbara Thatcher *Secretary* Maxine Willis *1st woman in evening gown* Ann Melton *2nd woman in evening gown* Ann Kramer *Showgirl* Carol Brewster *Secretary* Joann Arnold *Woman hotel guest* Marg Pemberton *Western Union girl* Ann Kimball *Bit girl* Kathy Case *Bit woman* Anne O'Neal *Bit man* Lester Dorr *Bit doorman* Jimmy Dundee *Old lady* Lillian West *Bit woman* Charlete Hardy *Bus driver* Sid Tomack *Man* Carry Owen *Adlib men* Tony Felice, Marty Rhiel, Buris De Jong, Gene Marshall *Adlib woman* Marie Allison *1st cop* Miles Shepart *2nd cop* Bob Thom *1st hot rod*

With Eddie Bracken and Barbara Lawrence.

Ann, Janet Leigh, Barbara Lawrence, Gloria De Haven, Tony Martin.

With Gloria De Haven and Barbara Lawrence.

passenger Ralph Hodges *2nd hot rod passenger* Michael Pierce *Bit showgirls* Shirley Buchanan, Mildred Carroll, Carmelita Eskew, Joanne Frank, Mary Ellen Gleason, Joan Jordan, Lola Kendrick, Shirley Kimball, Evelyn Lovequist, Kathleen O'Malley, June Paul, Marylin Symons, Beverly Thomas, Joan Whitney, Barbara Worthington *Bit girl* Eileen Coghlan *Beautiful girl* Suzanne Ames

CREDITS

Director: James V. Kern *Producer:* Howard Hughes *Dance numbers:* Busby Berkeley *Screenplay:* Sid Silvers, Hal Kanter *Based on a story by:* Sammy Cahn *Directors of photography:* Edward Cronjager, A.S.C. Harry J. Wild, A.S.C. *Technicolor consultant:* Morgan Padelford *Music score:* Walter Scharf *Art directors:* Albert S. D'Agostino, Carroll Clark *Set decorators:* Darrell Silvera, Harley Miller *Sound:* Earl Wolcott, Clem Portman *Gowns:* Michael Woulfe *Makeup:* Mel Berns *Hairstylist:* Larry Germain *Film editor:* Harry Marker *Running time:* 106 minutes.

SONGS

"Pelican Falls High," "Baby, You'll Never Be Sorry," "The Closer You Are," "Big Chief Hole-in-the-Ground," "Are You a Beautiful Dream?," "Let the Worry Bird Worry for You," "There's No Tomorrow," Prologue from *Pagliacci*, "Let's Make Comparisons," "Manhattan," "It Began in Yucatan."

SYNOPSIS

Everyone in Pelican Falls, Vermont, has come out to wish Nancy Peterson (Janet Leigh) bon voyage and good luck as she boards the bus to New York to embark on a theatrical career. Once aboard, she meets Hannah Holbrook (Gloria De Haven), Joyce Campbell (Ann Miller), and "Foxy" Rogers (Barbara Lawrence), an act on their way back to New York after flopping on a showboat. Their conniving and inept agent, Lew Conway (Eddie Bracken), also has singer Dan Carter (Tony Martin) on the string. Dan has decided to give up show business, but at the bus station, as the girls arrive, his luggage gets mixed up with Nancy's. He returns her baggage and stays on.

Lew has promised the young hopefuls a spot on the Bob Crosby TV show. In order to raise money for the act, he dupes delicatessen owners Harry and Leo (Joe Smith and Charles Dale). Lew, of course, can't even get an audition lined up with Bob Crosby, for, even when disguised, he can't get past the studio guards.

Meanwhile the act keeps rehearsing, and Nancy, feeling she has made it, notifies the Pelican Falls newspaper that she will be on television. Lew hires a has-been actor, Willard Glendon (Taylor Holmes), to impersonate Bob Crosby's manager and gets the group to perform at a benefit where, Lew assures them, Crosby will see their work. When it becomes obvious that Lew has tricked them again, Nancy believes that Dan has been in on it, too, and packs her bags to go back home.

Dan gets in to see Crosby and explains what has happened. Crosby decides to use the act on the show that very night. With not a moment to lose before airtime, Lew goes after Nancy and convinces her that they really are to be on Crosby's show. With the help of a sailor (Buddy Baer), he gets the bus turned around and headed for the TV studio. Nancy and Lew arrive in the nick of time.

CRITICAL REACTION

The *Hollywood Reporter:*
"*Two Tickets to Broadway* is an enchanting Technicolor musical . . . packed with bouncing good humor and an array of specialties encompassing virtually everything in the revue book. The handsome Howard Hughes presentation is a frank, unashamed musical reminiscent of those we enjoyed in the thirties. The emphasis is all on the numbers [and] the to-

"The Worry Bird"

Janet Leigh, Ann, Tony Martin, Barbara Lawrence, Gloria De Haven:
"Big Chief Hole-in-the-Ground."

tal effect is breathtaking. Ann Miller's rhythmic perfection is, as always, a delight."

Daily Variety:

"Prospects are bright for *Two Tickets to Broadway* . . . the combination of good humor, a score that registers easily, and a lush Technicolor dressing. There's top support from the Misses De Haven and Lawrence, and some flashing footwork by Ann Miller."

A. H. Weiler
in the *New York Times:*

"Broadway has been exposed to the likes of *Two Tickets to Broadway* many times before. This time, the experience is just a mite more cheerful than usual. The cast is energetic in trying to keep things moving. The producers have filled the screen with enough pulchritude to excite even the most hardened

misanthrope. There is a comic, eye-opening and stunt-filled turn by The Charlivels. But Janet Leigh, as Tony Martin's romantic vis-à-vis; Gloria De Haven, as Bracken's singing girl friend, and Ann Miller, as the tap dancing member of the team, personify the film's major attraction. The tunes in *Two Tickets to Broadway* may not generate much whistling, but the girls will."

The *New York Post:*

"Eddie Bracken, a prevaricating actor's agent, is peddling the talents of singer Tony Martin, dancer Ann Miller, singer Gloria De Haven, and looker Barbara Lawrence. They all move rapidly enough to preserve an appearance of liveliness. I guess that's at least bogey for the short, practice course of the variety-musical-comedy-romance that offers a little of everything and everything rather little."

Release date: July, 1952

CAST

Stephanie	KATHRYN GRAYSON
Al Marsh	RED SKELTON
Tony Naylor	HOWARD KEEL
Clarisse	MARGE CHAMPION
Jerry Ralby	GOWER CHAMPION
Bubbles Cassidy	ANN MILLER
Zsa Zsa	Zsa Zsa GABOR
Max Fogelsby	Kurt KASZNAR
Pierre	Marcel Dalio
Diane	Diane Cassidy

CREDITS

Director: Mervyn LeRoy *Producer*: Jack Cummings *Screenplay*: George Wells, Harry Ruby *Additional dialogue*: Andrew Solt Based on the musical comedy *Roberta From the novel* by Alice Duer Miller *Book and lyrics*: Otto A. Harbach *Music*: Jerome Kern *Additional and revised lyrics*: Dorothy Fields *Musical directors*: Carmen Dragon, Saul Chaplin *Choreography*: Hermes Pan *Orchestrations*: Leo Arnaud *Vocal arrangements*: Robert Tucker *Gowns*: Adrian *Director of photography*: George J. Fosley, A.S.C. *Technicolor consultants*: Henri Jaffa, James Gooch *Art directors*: Cedric Gibbons, Gabriel Scognamillo *Recording supervisor*: Douglas Shearer *Set decorators*: Edwin B. Willis, Jack D. Moore; *Fashion show*: Tony Duquette *Special effects*: A. Arnold Gillespie *Hairstyles*: Sydney Guilaroff *Make-up*: William Tuttle *Film editor*: John McSweeney, Jr. *Running time*: 103 minutes.

SONGS

"Opening Night," "I'll Be Hard to Handle," "You're Devastating," "I Won't Dance," "Lafayette," "Yesterdays," "Lovely to Look At," "Smoke Gets in Your Eyes," "The Most Exciting Night," "The Touch of Your Hand."

With Red Skelton.

SYNOPSIS

Al Marsh (Red Skelton), Tony Naylor (Howard Keel) and Jerry Ralby (Gower Champion) are unable to get financial backing for a new Broadway show. Bubbles Cassidy (Ann Miller), a showgirl who likes Naylor, offers them her life savings, but they turn her down. Marsh then learns that his Aunt Roberta has died and left him a half-interest in Roberta's, her Paris dress salon. The three friends leave for Paris, hoping to sell Marsh's interest in the shop to raise money for the show.

When they arrive, Stephanie (Kathryn Grayson) and Clarisse (Marge Champion), sisters adopted by Aunt Roberta, and the inheritors of the other half-interest in Roberta's, inform them that the shop is nearly bankrupt. Naylor has an idea for reviving the shop's popularity: a musical fashion show with the famed American designer Adrian creating some startling new gowns.

He then persuades the shop's creditors to put up new money for the fashion show. He also falls in love with Stephanie. Bubbles, who has arrived from the States, is annoyed. Another romance is beginning between Clarisse and Ralby, while Marsh carries a torch for Stephanie.

During rehearsals for the fashion show, one of the models, Zsa Zsa (Zsa Zsa Gabor) introduces her rich, elderly boy friend Max Fogelsby (Kurt Kasznar) to Naylor. Fogelsby is a Broadway producer who is willing to back their show on condition that the group leave immediately for New York.

Marsh, Ralby, and Bubbles are unwilling to let Stephanie and Clarisse down and refuse Fogelsby's offer. However, Naylor does return to New York but realizes he can't work on the show. Fogelsby then suggests that they return to Paris. They arrive in time to make the fashion show opening a huge success. Stephanie is now convinced that Naylor loves her after all, and Marsh and Bubbles find solace with each other.

CRITICAL REACTION

Daily Variety:

"That sterling musical comedy of yesteryear, *Roberta*, comes again to the screen as light, pleasant entertainment. The elaborate production flash provided by Jack Cummings and director Mervyn LeRoy help make this an above-average musical. Miss Miller displays talented feet and shapely gams in wrapping up a song and dance stint on 'I'll Be Hard to Handle.' Miss Miller is good."

A. H. Weiler in the *New York Times*:

"It is pleasing to report that the vehicle [*Roberta*] is a durable one and that the touch of Jerome Kern's hand is still magical. While the

With Red Skelton, Howard Keel, and Gower Champion.

"I'll Be Hard to Handle"

yarn was not a sparkling gem in the first place, *Lovely to Look At* [is] a shade duller than the original. But that is carping over what is essentially a trifling matter. Hermes Pan has inventively devised turns for 'I Won't Dance' and 'Smoke Gets in Your Eyes' to which Marge and Gower Champion contribute professional grace, verve and charm. And Ann Miller is permitted to exhibit both her beautiful legs and her staccato tapping in a snappy run through of 'I'll Be Hard to Handle.' The designer (Adrian) has a field day in the finale with enough new fashions to turn the head of a princess or a pauper. That, and the songs, should excite every distaff customer in the house and undoubtedly the gentlemen will go for it too. But watch out for that plot!"

Otis L. Guernsey, Jr., in the
New York Herald Tribune:
"A dim reminiscence of the musical *Roberta* is back on the screen, at Radio City Music Hall, under the heading of *Lovely to Look At*. The humor is forced, the high-fashion pageantry is elaborately dull, the color almost scorches the eyeball while only the melody lingers on. Red Skelton does a solo take-off on an Irish tenor and pairs off with tap dancer Ann Miller at the end. A passing good word must be said for the design of the masks and costumes of attendants looking like gargoyles in the fashion show scene. The occasional reward is meager, though, and is seldom in evidence through the gaudy doing of *Lovely to Look At*."

Release date: April 10, 1953

CAST

Cindy Kimbell . . . . JANE POWELL
Rick Belrow Livingston . . . . FARLEY GRANGER
Lisa Bellmount . . . . Ann MILLER
Eric Schlemmer . . . . S. Z. SAKALL
Judge Gordon Kimbell . . . . Robert KEITH
Himself . . . . Nat "King" COLE
Mrs. Livingston . . . . Billie BURKE
Ludwig Schlemmer . . . . Bobby VAN
Jailer . . . . Chill Wills
Mrs. Gordon Kimbell . . . . Fay Wray
Mac . . . . Dean Miller

Ted	William Campbell
Hemmingway	Philip Tonge
Jim, the cop	Jonathan Colt
Dennis	Bobby Hyatt
Jimmy	Rudy Lee
Deidre	Beverly Wills
Patsy	Gloria Noble
Betty	Jane Liddell
Mary	Nancy Valentine
Sandra	Janet Stewart
Susie	Pegi McIntire
Girl friend	Virginia Hall

CREDITS

Director: Leslie Kardos *Producer:* Joe Pasternak *Screenplay:* Dorothy Cooper, Dorothy Kingsley *Story:* Dorothy Cooper *Musical director:* Andre Previn *Musical numbers staged by:* Busby Berkeley *Vocal supervision:* Jeff Alexander *Director of photography:* Joseph Ruttenberg, A.S.C. *Technicolor consultants:* Henri Jaffa, Robert Brower *Art directors:* Cedric Gibbons, Hans Peters *Assistant director:* Bert Glazer *Recording supervisor:* Douglas Shearer *Set decorators:* Edwin B. Willis, Emile Kuri *Montage sequence:* Peter Ballbusch *Costumes:* Helen Rose *Hairstyles:* Sydney Guilaroff *Makeup:* William Tuttle *Film editor:* Albert Akst, A.C.E. *Running time:* 93 minutes.

SONGS

Music: Nicholas Brodszky; *lyrics:* Leo Robin. "My Flaming Heart," "Small Towns are Smile Towns," "The Lullaby of the Lord," "My Gaucho," "I've Gotta Hear That Beat," "Take Me to Broadway (Hippity Hop)," "Fine, Fine, Fine," "The Fellow I'd Follow."

SYNOPSIS

Rick Belrow Livingston (Farley Granger) is eloping with Lisa Bellmount (Ann Miller), a glamorous Broadway star. He speeds through a small town, Duck Creek, and Judge Gordon Kimbell (Robert Keith) sentences him to thirty days in jail. Livingston's protests are in

"I've Got to Hear That Beat"

vain. While he is in jail Livingston begins to like the town and the Judge's daughter, Cindy (Jane Powell).

However, he is eager to be with Lisa on her birthday. Livingston tells Cindy that it is his mother's birthday, so she persuades Happy (Chill Wills), the jailer, to let him out just for that night, but she insists on going with him.

At Livingston's home he eludes Cindy and rushes to Lisa's theater. When he returns he learns that Cindy has accidentally locked herself in the fur vault. He persuades Cindy to see something of New York's night life after thawing her out and wrapping her in his mother's mink coat. While dancing with Livingston, Cindy knows that she is in love.

The next day Livingston is safely back in jail, but the gossip in Duck Creek is about Cindy's escapade. Eric Schlemmer (S. Z. Sakall), the local druggist, is very worried. He hopes that Cindy and his son Ludwig (Bobby Van) will marry. Schlemmer ignores the fact that Ludwig's heart is set on a Broadway career. Schlemmer's persistence results in Livingston's parole, and he returns to Lisa in New York.

The following Sunday everyone is in church. A car is heard speeding through Duck Creek. The patrolman (Jonathan Colt) brings in Livingston and his mother (Billie Burke).

Cindy, who is singing in the choir, knows everything is going to be all right as her family welcomes the latecomers.

CRITICAL REACTION

Brog. in *Variety*:

"*Small Town Girl* packages an engaging round of light musical comedy offering fun, familiar names, Technicolor, and spritely songs and dances. Shapely Ann Miller exposes her 3-D gams in two hot production pieces, 'I've Gotta Hear That Beat,' flashily staged by Busby Berkeley, and 'My Gaucho,' a piece of south-of-the-border rhythm that she makes pay off. Situations laced through the plot are amusing and the music and dances appealing."

Howard Thompson in the *New York Times*:

"Admirers of Jane Powell, Farley Granger and those untiring pastel musical comedy romances from the Metro-Goldwyn-Mayer Technicolor assembly line should have little difficulty taking *Small Town Girl*, the latest, well in stride. Joe Pasternak, the producer, has mechanized a dandy array of talent along a wholesome but standard line. Fortunately, the musical sequences that unfurl at the drop of a cliché, are performed and staged with shiny competence. Two are dandies. With the terp-

"I've Got to Hear That Beat"

"My Gaucho"

sichorean turns of Ann Miller and a gangly youth named Bobby Van, the picture gets some sizzling artificial respiration. Perfectly cast as a peppery Rialto gold digger, Miss Miller turns one tap routine, in which she circumvents a spectacular stageful of weird instrumental decor, into a personal rhapsody."

Joe Pihodna in the
New York Herald Tribune:

"It is pleasant to report that the latest Joe Pasternak musical *Small Town Girl* has cheerful tunes, good-looking girls and enough laughs to make things run smoothly. Mr. Pasternak and M-G-M have thrown in everything to make sure the production runs according to schedule. The whole film is brightened by the individual performances of the featured players. Miss Miller, one of the most energetic dancers around, is the star of two colorful numbers done in the gaudiest cinema style. *Small Town Girl* is a relaxing hour and a half in the movies. No strain involved like getting up and turning the dial."

KISS ME KATE

Release date: November 26, 1953

CAST

Lilli Vanessi/"Katherine"	KATHRYN GRAYSON
Fred Graham/"Petruchio"	HOWARD KEEL
Lois Lane/"Bianca"	ANN MILLER
Lippy	Keenan WYNN
"Gremio"	Bobby VAN
Slug	James WHITMORE
"Baptista"	Kurt KASZNAR
Bill Calhoun/"Lucentio"	Tommy Rall
"Hortensio"	Bob Fosse
Cole Porter	Ron Randell
Tex Callaway	Willard Parker

Ralph . . . . Dave O'Brien
Paul . . . . Claud Allister
Suzanne . . . . Ann Codee
Specialty dancers . . . . Carol Haney, Jeanne Coyne

CREDITS

Director: George Sidney *Producer:* Jack Cummings *Screenplay:* Dorothy Kingsley *Based on the play produced on stage* by Lemuel Ayers, Arnold Saint Subber *Music and lyrics:* Cole Porter *Play* by Samuel and Bella Spewack *Musical directors:* Andre Previn, Saul Chaplin *Choreography:* Hermes Pan *Director of photography:* Charles Rosher, A.S.C. *Color consultant:* Alvord Eiseman *Art directors:* Cedric Gibbons, Urie McCleary *Assistant director:* George Rhein *Set decorators:* Edwin B. Willis, Richard Pefferle *Special effects:* Warren Newcombe *Costumes:* Walter Plunkett *Orchestrations:* Conrad Salinger, Skip Martin *Vocal supervision:* Robert Tucker *Recording supervisor:* Douglas Shearer *Hairstyles:* Sydney Guilaroff *Makeup:* William Tuttle *Film editor:* Ralph E. Winters, A.C.E. *Running Time:* 109 minutes.

SONGS

"Too Darn Hot," "So in Love," "We Open in Venice," "Always True to You—in My Fashion," "Why Can't You Behave?," "Where Is the Life That Late I Led?" "Brush Up Your Shakespeare," "Kiss Me Kate," "Tom, Dick or Harry," "I Hate Men," "Wunderbar," "I've Come to Wive It Wealthily in Padua," "Were Thine That Special Face," "From This Moment On."

With Cole Porter and Bob Fosse.

With Ron Randell, Kathryn Grayson, and Howard Keel:
"It's Too Darn Hot."

With Tommy Rall: "Why Can't You Behave?"

SYNOPSIS

For a musical, based on *The Taming of the Shrew* and entitled *Kiss Me Kate*, composer Cole Porter (Ron Randell) and actor-director Fred Graham (Howard Keel) want Lilli Vanessi (Kathryn Grayson), his ex-wife, for the leading role of "Katherine." She arrives at Graham's apartment to hear the score.

Copa star Lois Lane (Ann Miller), Graham's girl friend, bounces in and tells Lilli that she is playing "Bianca," Katherine's younger sister. Lilli refuses to do the show and says she is getting married. When Lois says that she can play Katherine, Lilli changes her mind quickly.

Rehearsals do not go smoothly, as Graham badgers Lilli. Lois's dancing partner, Bill Calhoun (Tommy Rall), who plays "Lucentio" in the show, is late for rehearsal. He has been gambling and has signed Graham's name to an I.O.U. for two thousand dollars.

On opening night two gangsters, Lippy (Keenan Wynn) and Slug (James Whitmore) confront Graham with the I.O.U., but he denies that his signature is on the chit.

Paul (Claud Allister), Graham's butler, gives Lilli's maid Suzanne (Ann Codee) flowers for Lilli, not realizing that the bouquet was meant for Lois. When Graham finds out, he tries to get his note from Lilli, but she tucks it into her bosom as the show starts.

In *Kiss Me Kate*, Bianca's three suitors, "Lucentio," "Gremio" (Bobby Van) and "Hortensio" (Bob Fosse) must wait until a mate is found for the shrewish Katherine. Graham, playing "Petruchio," a friend of Lucentio, arrives from Verone and strikes a bargain with Katherine's father "Baptista" (Kurt Kasznar). During the show Lilli reads the note and discovers the truth about the flowers. She starts digressing from the script to get back at Graham. As the first-act curtain falls, Graham puts her over his knee and paddles her.

Lilli says she is leaving the show and calls Tex Callaway (Willard Parker) to tell him she will marry him that very night. Lois also persuades Calhoun to confess to Graham about the I.O.U.

When Lippy and Slug hear that Lilli is leaving the show and there won't be any money with which to pay off the debt if the show closes, they force her to stay and become her bodyguards on and off the stage as the second act starts.

When Callaway arrives backstage, Lois recognizes him as an old boy friend from Houston. Lippy telephones his boss, a Mr. Hogan, to report on their progress just as Hogan is being eliminated. The two gangsters leave, since the debt and their boss both have been cancelled. Lilli also leaves with Callaway.

Before she goes, Graham tells her that he loves her and that she belongs in the theater. During the finale, Graham tells Baptista that the understudy will be going on in Lilli's place. But Lilli, in a change of heart, appears to finish the show and to resume her relationship with her leading man.

CRITICAL REACTION

Daily Variety:

"*Kiss Me Kate* is a mighty slick filmusical treatment of the legit hit and should prove ticket-selling entertainment. Its fancy songs, dances, comedy and trouping come over in eye-ear dazzling fashion. Film was lensed as the first all-musical in 3-D, but is available standard. Either way, it stands up. The choice of stars Kathryn Grayson, Howard Keel and Ann Miller to tackle the top roles was excellent and they have never been better. While all of the production numbers come over strongly, some can be classed as sock and one as wow. The latter is Miss Miller's terp version of 'Too Darn Hot.' It almost is. 'From This Moment On,' a Porter tune not in the original, gets fine song and dance treatment from Miss Miller, Bob Fosse, Tommy Rall and Bobby Van, with a terp assist from Carol Haney and Jeanne Coyne."

Variety:

"Metro's reputation for turning out top-caliber musical pictures is further enhanced with *Kiss Me Kate*, an eminently satisfying collaboration of superior song, dance and comedy talents. Cast work is uniformly top-notch, the

Kiss Me Kate rehearsals.

performers endowing the film with a variety of skills that bring out the best of both book and music. Miss Miller does a tap single at the outset of the pic which is billed 'Too Darn Hot,' and this is a spectacular sizzler."

Bosley Crowther
in the *New York Times*:

"One of the years more magnificent musical films, *Kiss Me Kate*, came dancing and tumbling into the Music Hall yesterday. [It] is a beautifully staged, adroitly acted and really superbly sung affair—better, indeed, if one may say so, than the same frolic was on the stage. As the nightclub tap dancer turned Bianca, Ann Miller is a splay of nimble legs and amusingly casual inclinations in handling some of the offering's better songs. The hoofing she and Tommy Rall do to 'Why Can't You Behave?' brings a lift where the picture needs it, and when she and her 'suitors' charge in and knock off 'Tom Dick and Harry,' the scenery shakes and the spirits soar. Under George Sidney's direction, the whole thing moves with zest and grace. Don't wait to be invited. Accept the offer of the title posthaste."

Otis L. Guernsey, Jr., in the
New York Herald Tribune:

"The Music Hall's *Kiss Me Kate* is a ragged screen version of the Cole Porter stage musical—an indecisive piece of musical production, without style or rhythm. The double filming in 3-D and flat must account for some of the musical's awkwardness; clearly, there are many scenes here angled for 3-D. Even more important, the cast seems to have no grasp of the temperamental, waspish backstage comedy which helped to make *Kiss Me Kate* a roaring hit on Broadway. Ann Miller's specialty heel-tapping is racy and rhythmical, but it is staged as though she were a bystander trying to steal some footage by thrusting herself into camera range. Mr. Porter himself is rung in as a character played by Ron Randell, in the opening scene of this *Kiss Me Kate*. Like the screen version of his show, this screen version of his person is disappointing."

Kathryn Grayson, Tommy Rall, Ann, and Howard Keel: "We Open in Venice."

Ann, Tommy Rall, Bobby Van, Bob Fosse: "Tom Dick or Harry."

Kurt Kasznar, Bob Fosse, Bobby Van, Ann, Tommy Rall
look on while Howard Keel tames shrew Kathryn Grayson.

Release date: December 24, 1954

CAST

Sigmund Romberg	JOSE FERRER
Dorothy Donnelly	MERLE OBERON
Anna Mueller	HELEN TRAUBEL
Lillian Romberg	Doe AVEDON
Gaby Deslys	Tamara TOUMANOVA
Bert Townsend	Paul STEWART
Mrs. Harris	Isobel ELSOM
Lazar Berrison, Sr.	David Burns
Ben Judson	Jim Backus

Guest Stars

J. J. Shubert .... WALTER PIDGEON
Florenz Ziegfeld .... PAUL HENREID

And

ROSEMARY CLOONEY, GENE and FRED KELLY,
JANE POWELL, VIC DAMONE, *ANN MILLER*,
CYD CHARISSE, HOWARD KEEL, TONY MARTIN,
William OLVIS, James MITCHELL, Joan Weldon

CREDITS

Director: Stanley Donen *Producer:* Roger Edens *Screenplay:* Leonard Spigelgass *From the book by:* Elliot Arnold *Musical supervision and conductor:* Adolph Deutsch *Orchestrations:* Hugo Friedhofer, Alexander Courage *Vocal arrangements:* Robert Tucker *Director of photography:* George Folsey, A.S.C. *Color consultant:* Alvord Eiseman *Art directors:* Cedric Gibbons, Edward Carfagno *Set decorators:* Edwin B. Willis, Arthur Krams *Special effects:* Warren Newcombe *Choreography:* Eugene Loring *Assistant director:* Robert Vreeland *Makeup:* William Tuttle *Women's costumes:* Helen Rose *Men's costumes:* Walter Plunkett *Recording supervisor:* Wesley C. Miller *Hairstyles:* Sidney Guilaroff *Film editor:* Adrienne Fazan, A.C.E. *Running time:* 132 minutes.

SONGS

"When I Grow Too Old to Dream," "Goodbye Girls," "Mr. and Mrs.," "One Alone," "Maytime," "Softly as in a Morning Sunrise," "Fat, Fat Fatima," "Jazza, Jazza, Doo, Do," "Lover, Come Back to Me," "Serenade," "Will You Remember?," "Miss U.S.A.," "Leg of Mutton," "Stouthearted Men," "Road to Paradise," "One Kiss," "Auf Wiedersehn," "I Love to Go Swimmin' with Women," "Your Land and My Land," "It."

SYNOPSIS

Sigmund Romberg (Jose Ferrer) is the leader of a small orchestra at the Cafe Vienna. The New York café is run by his old friend from Vienna, Anna Mueller (Helen Traubel). Romberg wants to write music, but a theatrical agent thinks his "Oom-pa-pa" Viennese waltzes are old-fashioned. Romberg then writes his first popular song, "Leg of Mutton."

The song's popularity prompts Broadway star Gaby Deslys (Tamara Toumanova) to ask J. J. Shubert (Walter Pidgeon) to have Romberg compose something for her new show. Dorothy Donnelly (Merle Oberon) also tells Romberg that a Broadway show will give him style. Bert Townsend (Paul Stewart), Shubert's business manager, pays Romberg two hundred dollars for "Softly, as in a Morning Sunrise." Gaby uses the song as a "girly number" for the first act finale.

Later, at the cafe, Anna sings the song as it should be sung. Rombert is upset, but Dorothy convinces him to sign a contract and write the score for *Whirl of the World*. The show is a hit. Romberg then does *The Midnight Girl*, taking a turn with the star (Rosemary Clooney) when the tenor is incapacitated, singing "Mr. and Mrs." Romberg is becoming prosperous. *Dancing Around* with the O'Brien brothers (Gene and Fred Kelly) is next. They sing "I Love to Go Swimmin' with Women."

Shubert is not impressed with the score of *Maytime*, calling it "wiener schnitzel," but it is a huge hit featuring melodies like "Road to Paradise" (sung by Vic Damone) and "Will You Remember?" (sung by Jane Powell and Damone).

A flop, *Magic Melody*, makes Romberg realize that show business is made up of specialists and that he should stick to writing music. He goes to an upstate resort with Townsend and Ben Judson (Jim Backus) to work on a new show, *Jazz-a-Doo*.

"It"

At the resort he meets Lillian Harris (Doe Avedon) and her mother (Isobel Elsom). Mrs. Harris is shocked when she attends an audition of Romberg's new show.

Romberg composes "It" (sung and danced by Ann Miller) for *Artists and Models* and then, in collaboration with Dorothy, *The Student Prince*, with its haunting "Serenade" (sung by William Olvis). It seems that now everyone is singing Romberg's music.

Lillian becomes his wife. Romberg communicates theatrical excitement to her and she looks forward to the opening nights of *The Desert Song* (featuring "One Alone" sung and danced by Cyd Charisse and James Mitchell) and *My Maryland* (with "Your Land and My Land," sung by Howard Keel).

Dorothy becomes ill and dies. Her death is very hard on Romberg, but Lillian urges him to go back to work. This time, in collaboration with Oscar Hammerstein, the result is *New Moon* (Tony Martin and Joan Weldon perform "Lover, Come Back to Me").

Years later, at a symphony concert, Romberg pays tribute to Lillian and dedicates "When I Grow Too Old to Dream" to his wife.

CRITICAL REACTION

The *Hollywood Reporter:*
"For the public *Deep in My Heart* spells ENTERTAINMENT in capital letters. With a firmament of big name stars and some of the most ear-catching music ever written, it has the added advantage of hilarious routines of a quality seldom seen in a musical biography. There's a list of stars to fill any theater and an assemblage of melodic scores to set any audience dreaming. Each of these numbers is cast and presented with the care and skill that is usually reserved for the climax of the ordinary

screen musical. Each got an ovation at the preview."

Otis L. Guernsey, Jr., in the New York Herald Tribune:

"*Deep in My Heart* is right in step with the waltzy swing of the season. It is a musical biography of Sigmund Romberg, with a heap of songs and a ton of affection in Jose Ferrer's performance of the composer. There is no tension in it—it is two hours of schmaltz, and guest stars, and production and an airy little libretto crammed with Romberg music. Everywhere you go in this movie they're playing something from Romberg and the actors must either join the chorus or get out of the way of the parade of production numbers. Guest stars like Rosemary Clooney, Gene Kelly, Jane Powell, Ann Miller, Cyd Charisse and Tony Martin do single numbers from operettas like *Maytime, Artists and Models, The Desert Song*

and *New Moon. Deep in My Heart* is aimed at those who thirst for great gobbets of Romberg melody."

Bosley Crowther in the New York Times:

"This large potpourri of popular music has been dished up in color by Metro-Goldwyn-Mayer and is called *Deep in My Heart,* from the title of one of Mr. Romberg's juicier songs. This medly of melodies runs more to showy presentations of the more familiar of the composer's tunes than it does to a logical development of dramatic values in the life of the man. Ann Miller pops up in a take-off of the Twenties from *Artists and Models,* titled 'It.' Amidst all this disconnected vaudeville, it is small wonder that Mr. Ferrer is unable to make Sigmund Romberg any more than a mawkish platitude. Nor is any help forthcoming from the screenplay . . . It calls for a considerable tolerance for clichés."

Release date: March 4, 1955

CAST

Susan Smith	JANE POWELL
Chief boatswain's mate William F. Clark	TONY MARTIN
Carol Pace	DEBBIE REYNOLDS
Rear Admiral Daniel Xavier Smith	WALTER PIDGEON
Rico Ferrari	VIC DAMONE
Wendell Craig	GENE RAYMOND
Ginger	ANN MILLER
Danny Xavier Smith	RUSS TAMBLYN
Mrs. Ottavio Ferrari	Kay ARMEN
Mr. Peroni	J. Carrol NAISH
Lieutenant Jackson	Richard ANDERSON

Jenny	Jane DARWELL
Shore patrol	Alan King, Henry Slate
Themselves	Jubalaires
Dancer	Frank Reynolds

CREDITS

Director: Roy Rowland *Producer:* Joe Pasternak *Written by:* Sonya Levien, William Ludwig *Based on the musical play Hit the Deck* by Herbert Fields *Presented on stage by* Vincent Youmans *From Shore Leave* by Hubert Osborne *Music supervision and conductor:* George Stoll *Musical numbers staged by:* Hermes Pan *Director of photography:* George Folsey, A.S.C. *Art directors:* Cedric Gibbons, Paul Groesse *Color consultant:* Alvord Eiseman *Costumes:* Helen Rose *Orchestral arrangements:* Robert Van Eps, Will Beitel *Vocal supervision:* Jeff Alexander *Assistant director:* George Rhein *Recording supervisor:* Wesley C. Miller *Set decorators:* Edwin B. Willis, Fred MacLean *Hairstyles:* Sydney Guilaroff *Makeup:* William Tuttle *Film editor:* John McSweeney, Jr. *Running time:* 117 minutes.

SONGS

Music and lyrics: Vincent Youmans, Irving Caesar, Leo Robin, Clifford Grey, Anne Caldwell, Sidney Clare, A. Pestalozza, Howard Johnson, William Rose, Edward Eliscu. "Sometimes I'm Happy," "Join the Navy," "Loo-Loo," "Why, Oh, Why?," "Lucky Bird," "Lady from the Bayou," "A Kiss or Two," "Hallelujah," "I Know that You Know," "Keepin' Myself for You," "Ciribiribin," "More Than You Know."

SYNOPSIS

A sailor, Danny Xavier Smith (Russ Tamblyn), on leave, discovers his sister Susan (Jane Powell) all dolled up in a plunging red dress and ready to audition for a rich theatrical producer, Wendell Craig (Gene Raymond).

Smith follows Susan to the theater, where he sees Carol Pace (Debbie Reynolds) rehearsing a dance number in the show *Hit the Deck*. Smith joins in the number, "A Kiss or Two," which Carol is doing with chorus boys dressed as sailors.

Carol is angry, but when she learns that Smith has come to defend his sister's virtue she tells him that Craig auditions at his home and that everyone knows he is a wolf.

Chief boatswain's mate William F. Clark (Tony Martin) wants to resume his relation-

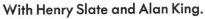

With Henry Slate and Alan King.

"Keepin' Myself for You"

ship with Ginger (Ann Miller), a nightclub dancer, but Ginger is getting tired of waiting six years for a marriage proposal. Smith asks his buddies, Clark and Rico Ferrari (Vic Damone) to help him save Susan, and the trio wreck Craig's elegant penthouse.

The Navy takes a dim view of this and sends out the shore patrol (Alan King and Henry Slate) to arrest the three sailors.

Smith, son of Rear Admiral Daniel Xavier Smith (Walter Pidgeon), hopes for an appointment to Annapolis; this escapade would ruin his good record and his chances for the appointment. Susan is also afraid to tell her father that she has fallen in love with Rico, particularly since he is both a sailor and on the lam.

But the three sailors do land in the brig. When Rear Admiral Smith learns of Susan's involvement in the affair, the charges are dropped. Love wins the day as Clark finally says yes to Ginger, and Susan and Rico and Carol and young Smith pair off.

CRITICAL REACTION

Wanda Hale in the New York Daily News: "Radio City Music Hall presents *Hit the Deck*, a large busy musical comedy with a large cast of popular entertainers filled with a large amount of Vincent Youmans' music. The energetic song and dance girls are Jane Powell, Debbie Reynolds and Ann Miller, the boys are Tony Martin, Vic Damone and Russ Tamblyn. Jane Powell and Tony Martin are entrusted, and rightly so, with the best of Youmans' compositions. But everybody sings, solo, duet and in chorus. Plot developments pause often for entertainment by the stars and the extras."

Jack Moffitt in the Hollywood Reporter: "With each of its nine leading parts played by a star of proven name value and with a great Vincent Youmans score adding the best of ear appeal, there is no lack of audience attraction. Ann Miller, as (Tony Martin's)

"Lady from the Bayou"

hard-boiled girl friend with the heart of gold, clicks off several of her familiar and popular tap routines. One of these, performed on a polished deck with a whole ship's company of fast-stepping chorus men in the background, is a terrific bit of nimble spectacle. But I liked her sultry and tropical barefoot 'Lady from the Bayou' even better because it lets her reveal a new and interesting personality and a dance routine that is, for her, something different. The success of this and the big naval tap routine is enhanced by the expert staging of Hermes Pan. All in all, it's an extremely pleasant picture."

A. H. Weiler in the *New York Times*:
"Although *Hit the Deck* which was unveiled at the Music Hall yesterday, is as full of pleasant sounds and frenzied movement as chow time on a battleship, it rarely satisfies a viewer hungry for originality. Loaded to the gunwales with the studio's eager young singing and dancing talent, who do justice to some noted tunes, it nevertheless emerges as a routine treatment. Producers and sailors have been known to be more inventive. As a night club's leading dancing doll, Ann Miller torridly undulates to the boogie beat of 'Lady from the Bayou' and she also earns her keep in a fast rattling climatic tap routine."

"Hallelujah!"

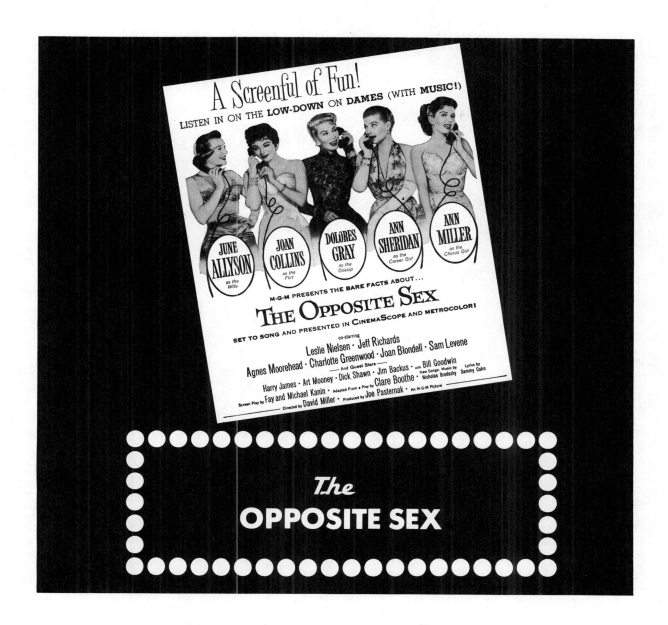

Release date: October 26, 1956

CAST

Kay	JUNE ALLYSON
Crystal Allen	JOAN COLLINS
Sylvia Fowler	DOLORES GRAY
Amanda Penrose	ANN SHERIDAN
Gloria Dell	ANN MILLER
Steve Hilliard	Leslie NIELSEN
Buck Winston	Jeff RICHARDS
Countess Lavaliere	Agnes MOOREHEAD
Lucy	Charlotte GREENWOOD
Edith Potter	Joan BLONDELL
Mike Pearl	Sam LEVENE

Ann, Dolores Gray, June Allyson, Ann Sheridan,
Joan Blondell, and Joan Collins.

Howard Fowler	Bill Goodwin
Olga	Alice Pearce
Dolly	Barbara Jo Allen
Debbie	Sandy Descher
Pat	Carolyn Jones
Leading man dancer	Jerry Antes
Ted	Alan Marshall
Phelps Potter	Jonathan Hole
Chorine	Darlene Engle
Dancer	Marc Wilder
Specialty act	Trio Ariston
Leg model	Marjorie Helen

Guest stars

Himself	HARRY JAMES
Himself	ART MOONEY
Singer	DICK SHAWN
Psychiatrist	JIM BACKUS

CREDITS

Director: David Miller *Producer:* Joe Pasternak *Screenplay:* Fay and Michael Kanin *Adapted from a play by:* Clare Boothe *Musical supervisor:* George Stoll *Dances and musical numbers:* Robert Sidney *Orchestrations:* Albert Sendrey, Skip Martin *Vocal supervision:* Robert Tucker *Music coordinator:* Irving Aaronson *Costumes:* Helen Rose *Director of photography:* Robert Bronner, A.S.C. *Art directors:* Cedric Gibbons, Daniel B. Cathcart *Set decorator:* Edwin B. Willis *Special effects:* A. Arnold Gillespie, Warren Newcombe *Assistant director:* George Rhein *Color consultant:* Charles K. Hagedon *Recording supervisor:* Dr. Wesley C. Miller *Hairstyles:* Sydney Guilaroff *Makeup:* William Tuttle *Film editor:* John McSweeney, Jr. *Running time:* 117 minutes.

SONGS

Music and lyrics: Nicolas Brodszky, Sammy Cahn, George Stoll, Ralph Freed. "The Opposite Sex," "Dere's Yellow Gold on De Trees (De Banana)," "A Perfect Love," "Rock and Roll Tumbleweed," "Now! Baby, Now!," "Jungle Red," "Young Man with a Horn."

SYNOPSIS

Kay Hilliard (June Allyson) and her husband, Broadway producer Steve Hilliard (Leslie Nielsen), are celebrating their tenth wedding anniversary. Kay has never regretted giving up her singing career to be a wife and mother to seven-year-old Debbie (Sandy Descher).

At her anniversary dinner, her supposed good friend Sylvia Fowler (Dolores Gray) plants the seeds of distrust in her mind. Olga (Alice Pearce), a gossiping manicurist, confirms the rumor that Hilliard is having an affair with showgirl Crystal Allen (Joan Collins).

Against the advice of two sympathetic friends, Amanda Penrose (Ann Sheridan) and Edith Potter (Joan Blondell), Kay goes to Reno for a divorce. At the guest ranch of Lucy (Charlotte Greenwood) she becomes friendly with chorusgirl Gloria Dell (Ann Miller) and the Countess Lavaliere (Agnes Moorehead).

Who should turn up but Sylvia, who has lost her husband to Gloria and has now turned her interest to a singing cowboy, Buck Winston (Jeff Richards).

After the divorce, Kay resumes her singing career and Hilliard marries Crystal. Sylvia, meanwhile, has brought Winston back with

The fight scene.

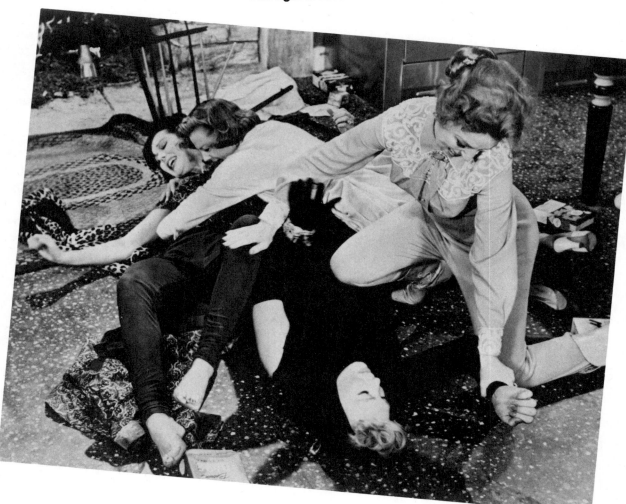

her and is launching him as a nightclub singer. Kay learns that Crystal is now cheating on Hilliard with the cowboy, and Kay is determined to win her ex-husband back.

With the help of Dolly (Barbara Jo Allen), a Broadway columnist, she exposes Crystal. Crystal discovers that Winston is not the marrying kind. But Kay and Hilliard are.

CRITICAL REACTION

Variety:

"As a remake with music of Clare Boothe's feline comedy, *The Women*, first screened by Metro in 1939, *The Opposite Sex* is high-powered entertainment with a name cast and a strong boxoffice potential. The mixture of marriage and morals, songs and satire, plays with a pleasant frothy glibness as the femmes test their claws on each other and on their men. In addition to the tune ditties, Miss Allyson clicks as the ever-loving wife [and] gets Nielsen in an exposé of feline tricks-of-the-trade that gain in mirth under such instructors as Dolores Gray, a dame who loses Bill Goodwin to the non-dancing but potent Ann Miller."

A. H. Weiler in the *New York Times:*

"Most of Miss Boothe's comedy-drama still drips vitriol and the fangs and claws of its decorative vixens are almost as terrifying as they were two decades ago. One might not want to live in this plush 'jungle' but the principals, who keep the catfights going briskly, make it an interesting place to visit. The lush wardrobes, enhanced by excellent color photography provided for this covey of dames, is enough to drive distaff viewers to distraction. Dolores Gray, as the blonde gossipmonger who loses her mate to Ann Miller, [and] Ann Sheridan, Joan Blondell and Agnes Moorehead lend spice to the palaver and punch to the battles. The ladies dominate *The Opposite Sex*. It should be a treat for them."

Joe Pihodna in the *New York Herald Tribune:*

"M-G-M has made a lucious musical out of the acid comedy-drama, *The Women*. The studio has taken some of the bite out of the bitter portraits of idle, gossiping women by dressing the play with music and color. Dolores Gray plays the most despicable of the buzzards. Also she plays the role of the heroine's worst best friend with a chilling conviction which is a tribute to her acting ability. Ann Sheridan, Ann Miller, Agnes Moorehead and Joan Blondell form a smart, well-dressed set of ladies who live luxuriously in the best M-G-M tradition."

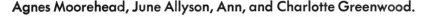

Agnes Moorehead, June Allyson, Ann, and Charlotte Greenwood.

Release date: December 7, 1956

CAST

Bruce Hallerton	TOM EWELL
Betty Hallerton	ANNE FRANCIS
Mrs. Doris Patterson	ANN MILLER
Buck Rivers	Dean Jones
Dennis Hallerton	Rudy Lee
Ed Ryder	Judson Pratt
George Carruthers	Raymond Bailey
Mr. Dawson	Wilfred Knapp
Mr. O'Keefe	Bob Jellison
Man Mountain O'Keefe	Todd Ferrell
Herbie Patterson	Raymond Winston

Foster Carruthers	Paul Engle
Mrs. George Carruthers	Ann Morriss
Samuel J. Garway	Gene O'Donnell
Himself	"Smidgeon" the Dog
Extra	Nathaniel Benchley

CREDITS

Director: Herman Hoffman *Producer:* Henry Berman *Written by:* Nathaniel Benchley *Music:* Jeff Alexander *Director of photography:* Arthur E. Arling, A.S.C. *Art directors:* William A. Horning, Randall Duell *Set decorators:* Edwin B. Willis, Edward G. Boyle *Special effects:* A. Arnold Gillespie *Assistant director:* George Rhein *Recording supervisor:* Dr. Wesley C. Miller *Makeup:* William Tuttle *Film editor:* Gene Ruggiero, A.C.E. *Running time:* 89 minutes.

SYNOPSIS

Bruce Hallerton (Tom Ewell) has a prosperous law business and a contented family life. With his wife, Betty (Anne Francis), son, Dennis (Rudy Lee), a typical American boy, and the Yankees on a winning streak, he is happy. But he doesn't know when he's well off.

The Panthers, a little-league baseball team sadly in need of pitchers and hitters, also needs a coach. Hallerton lets himself be talked into the position. The team is a loser and Hallerton is in the doghouse.

To complicate matters, Mrs. Doris Patterson (Ann Miller), an attractive widow, has a son, Herbie (Raymond Winston), who is on the little league team. Hallerton suspects that Doris has romantic designs on him and that her outward interest in baseball is just a cover-up. Doris shows up for every game and

With Tom Ewell.

With Tom Ewell.

cordially invites the coach to drop by her house after the game. Betty becomes very jealous.

When Hallerton accuses Doris of trying to wreck his home life, she tells him off. Doris has never had any interest in him personally. Her only interest was in her son and his baseball playing. With this, Hallerton's ego is shattered.

He finally manages to whip the Panthers into shape and they win the league championship. The now successful baseball coach embarks on a new career as a Cub Scout leader!

CRITICAL REACTION

Brog. in *Daily Variety:*

"*The Great American Pastime* is a family-type comedy built around Little League baseball. Tom Ewell injects chuckles into a number of situations via his deft timing and facial mugging. Anne Francis scores strongly as his suffering wife. Ann Miller does okay as a pretty young widow whom Ewell fancies has fallen for him, while actually she's only trying to look after the interests of her son. The others in the cast all play it free and easy. Jeff Alexander's score does its share in helping the amusement."

The *Hollywood Reporter:*

"*The Great American Pastime* is little-league baseball. Of course, the title was chosen for its possible double meaning and it is a persuasive designation for a captivating family comedy. Tom Ewell is the closest thing we have today to the late Robert Benchley [with] the same ability to render a flat line with humorous effect. Miss Francis is lovely, as always. Ann Miller is a good-natured female menace."

Holl. in *Variety:*

"What this country needs is more family pictures with American themes. At least that's the sentiment of a segment of exhibitors. Metro's *The Great American Pastime* fulfills both requirements. There are a number of amusing incidents in the Nathaniel Benchley comedy and the story of little-league baseball will be probably close to many family groups. For the most part, though, *The Great American Pastime* appears to be headed for double-feature situations. Tom Ewell is frequently funny in a farcical way but his character never emerges as a real person. Miss Miller is okay as the young widow and the young little leaguers, portrayed by Rudy Lee, Raymond Winston, and Todd Ferrell, are properly confused by the antics of their parents."

Release date: May, 1974

SPECIAL APPEARANCES

FRED ASTAIRE, BING CROSBY, GENE KELLY,
PETER LAWFORD, LIZA MINNELLI, DONALD O'CONNOR,
DEBBIE REYNOLDS, MICKEY ROONEY, FRANK SINATRA,
JAMES STEWART, ELIZABETH TAYLOR

CREDITS

Written, produced, directed by: Jack Haley, Jr. *Executive producer:* Daniel Melnick *Additional music adapted by:* Henry Mancini *Film editor:* Bud Friedgen, A.C.E. *Co-film editor:* David E. Blewitt, A.C.E. *Running time:* 132 minutes. *An M-G-M Picture. Released by* United Artists, a Transamerica Company.

SYNOPSIS

1

Frank Sinatra, narrator: "Singin' in the Rain," *Hollywood Revue of 1929*, Cliff "Ukelele Ike" Edwards; *Speak Easily*, Jimmy Durante; *Little Nellie Kelly*, Judy Garland, *Singin' in the Rain*, Gene Kelly, Debbie Reynolds, Donald O'Connor; "Broadway Melody," *Broadway Melody of 1929*, Charles King; "Rosalie," *Rosalie*, Eleanor Powell; "Indian Love Call," *Rose Marie*, Jeanette MacDonald, Nelson Eddy; "A Pretty Girl Is Like a Melody," *The Great Ziegfeld*, Dennis Morgan (sung by Allan Jones), Virginia Bruce; "Begin the Beguine," *Broadway Melody of 1940*, Fred Astaire, Eleanor Powell; "The Song's Gotta Come from the Heart," *It Happened in Brooklyn*, Jimmy Durante, Frank Sinatra.

2

Elizabeth Taylor, narrator: "The Music of Spring," *Cynthia*, Elizabeth Taylor; "Honeysuckle Rose," *Thousands Cheer*, Lena Horne; "Take Me Out to the Ball Game," *Take Me Out to the Ball Game*, Frank Sinatra, Gene Kelly; "Thou Swell," *Words and Music*, June Allyson, The Blackburn Twins; "The Varsity Drag," *Good News*, June Allyson, Peter Lawford.

3

Peter Lawford, narrator: "Pagan Number," *On an Island with You*, Jimmy Durante, Peter Lawford; "Abba Dabba Honeymoon," *Two Weeks with Love*, Debbie Reynolds, Carlton Carpenter; "It's a Most Unusual Day," *A Date with Judy*, Elizabeth Taylor, Jane Powell, Scotty Beckett, cast; "On the Atchison, Topeka, and the Sante Fe," *The Harvey Girls*, Judy Garland.

4

James Stewart, narrator: "It Must Be You," *Free and Easy*, Robert Montgomery; "Did You Ever," *Hollywood Revue*, Joan Crawford; "Reckless," *Reckless*, Jean Harlow; "Did I Remember?," *Susie*, Cary Grant; "You'd Be So Easy to Love," *Born to Dance*, James Stewart, Eleanor Powell; "Puttin' on the Ritz," *Idiot's Delight*, Clark Gable; "You Made Me Love You" ("Dear Mr. Gable"), *Broadway Melody of 1938*, Judy Garland.

5

Mickey Rooney, narrator: "Tap number," *Broadway to Hollywood*, Mickey Rooney; Judy Garland and Mickey Rooney montage from *Andy Hardy*, *Babes in Arms*, *Babes on Broadway*, *Strike Up the Band*, *Girl Crazy*.

6

Gene Kelly, narrator: "The Babbitt and the Bromide," *Ziegfeld Follies*, Fred Astaire, Gene Kelly; "They Can't Take That Away from Me," *The Barkleys of Broadway*, Fred Astaire, Ginger Rogers; "Heigh Ho, the Gang's All Here," *Dancing Lady*, Joan Crawford, Fred Astaire; "I Guess I'll Have to Change My Plan," *The Bandwagon*, Fred Astaire, Jack Buchanan; "Hat Rack Dance," *Royal Wedding*, Fred Astaire; "I've Got Shoes with Wings On," *The Barkleys of Broadway*, Fred Astaire; "Ceiling Dance," *Royal Wedding*, Fred Astaire; "Dancing in the Dark," *The Bandwagon*, Fred Astaire, Cyd Charisse.

7

Donald O'Connor, narrator: Esther Williams swimming montage, including scenes from *Bathing Beauty*, *Neptune's Daughter*, *On an Island With You*, *Dangerous When Wet*, *Thrill of a Romance*, and *Million Dollar Mermaid* with co-stars Howard Keel, Fernando Lamas, Van Johnson, Peter Lawford, Ricardo Montalban, Tom and Jerry, Jimmy Durante, Red Skelton; *I Love Melvin*, Debbie Reynolds.

8

Debbie Reynolds, narrator: "I Wanna Be Loved by You," *Three Little Words*, Fred Astaire, Red Skelton, Debbie Reynolds, Carlton Carpenter; "I Gotta Hear That Beat," *Small Town Girl*, Ann Miller; "Be My Love," *The Toast of New Orleans*, Kathryn Grayson, Mario Lanza; "Make 'Em Laugh," *Singin' in the Rain*, Donald O'Connor; "Cotton Blossom," "Make Believe," "Old Man River," *Show Boat*, Chorus, Kathryn Grayson, Howard Keel, William Warfield, Ava Gardner; "I'll Go My Way by Myself," *The Bandwagon*, Fred Astaire.

9

Fred Astaire, narrator: "Be a Clown," *The Pirate*, Gene Kelly, The Nicholas Brothers;

"I've Got to Hear That Beat"

Living in a Big Way, Gene Kelly; "Pirate Ballet," *The Pirate*, Gene Kelly; *Anchors Aweigh*, Gene Kelly; "New York, New York," *On the Town*, Frank Sinatra, Gene Kelly, Jules Munshin; *Anchors Aweigh*, Gene Kelly, Jerry the Mouse; "Singin' in the Rain," "Broadway Ballet Finale," *Singin' in the Rain*, Gene Kelly, Dicki Lerner, Cyd Charisse, chorus.

10

Liza Minnelli, narrator: "In the Good Old Summertime," *In the Good Old Summertime*, Judy Garland, Van Johnson, Liza Minnelli; "La Cucaracha, (*La Fiesta Santa Barbara*,)" The Gumm Sisters; "Americana," *Every Sunday*, Judy Garland, Deanna Durbin; *Broadway Melody of 1938*, Buddy Ebsen, Judy Garland; "Over the Rainbow," Medley, *Wizard of Oz*, Judy Garland, Ray Bolger, Jack Haley, Bert Lahr; "But Not for Me," *Girl Crazy*, Judy Garland; "The Trolley Song," *Meet Me in Saint Louis*, Judy Garland; "Under the Bamboo Tree," *Meet Me in Saint Louis*, Margaret O'Brien, Judy Garland; "The Boy Next Door," *Meet Me in Saint Louis*, Judy Garland; "Get Happy," *Summer Stock*, Judy Garland.

11

Bing Crosby, narrator: "Going Hollywood," *Going Hollywood*, Bing Crosby; "What a

"Hallelujah!"

Swell Party This Is," *High Society*, Bing Crosby, Frank Sinatra; "True Love," *High Society*, Bing Crosby, Grace Kelly; "Hallelujah!" *Hit The Deck*, Kay Armen, Tony Martin, Vic Damone, Debbie Reynolds, Jane Powell, Ann Miller; "Barn Raising Ballet," *Seven Brides for Seven Brothers*; "Gigi," *Gigi*, Louis Jourdan; "I Remember it Well," *Gigi*, Hermione Gingold, Maurice Chevalier; "Thank Heaven for Little Girls," *Gigi*, Maurice Chevalier.

12

Frank Sinatra, narrator: "Ballet," *An American in Paris*, Gene Kelly, Leslie Caron, ensemble.

CRITICAL REACTION

Ann Guarino in the *New York Daily News:*
"For real nostalgia *That's Entertainment!* at the Ziegfeld can't be beat—a fabulous compilation of highlights from numerous musicals made by Metro-Goldwyn-Mayer from 1929 to 1958. The vitality, youth, freshness of young performers like Garland, Mickey Rooney, Lana Turner, Ann Miller, Eleanor Powell, and Esther Williams are captured on screen. Everyone should see this film. It is tops in entertainment."

Archer Winsten in the *New York Post:*
"For the young who don't know what magnificence used to pour out of MGM, the film can be a revelation. For those who are old enough to remember, it's a fine rich trip down one part of celluloid Memory Lane."

Murf. in *Variety:*
"While many ponder the future of M-G-M, nobody can deny that it has had one hell of a past. The 50-year-old company is celebrating the anniversary with *That's Entertainment!*, an outstanding, stunning, sentimental, exciting, colorful, enjoyable, spirit-lifting, tuneful, youthful, invigorating, zesty, respectful, heartwarming, awesome, cheerful, dazzling and richly satisfying feature documentary commemorating its filmusicals. *That's Entertainment!* more than lives up to its name."

Roger Dooley in the *Villager:*
"What could be nearer a movie buff's dream than all the best numbers from all the best M-G-M musicals? It's a giant box of bon-bons that never becomes cloying because it is held together by a series of introductions and bridging commentaries delivered with wry humor and bittersweet reminiscence by eleven MGM veterans. *That's Entertainment!* lives brilliantly up to its name."

Benny Green in *Punch:*
"*That's Entertainment!* is irresistible. I discover, for example, that for a quarter of a century, I have, all unwittingly, been conversant with the vocal techniques of Margaret O'Brien, the lower thighs of Ann Miller, the timbre of Joan Crawford's voice. *That's Entertainment!* will please more people than any film for years. Everyone will surely find some favorite sequence left out. I am pleased to report for my own part, that the Garland and Gable montages are deeply moving, that Rooney and Durante and the gangling Sinatra and the juvenile Cary Grant and the boyish James Stewart and the frail ghost of Harlow and those thighs of Ann Miller all retain their appeal. In fact *That's Entertainment!* is not a masterpiece so much as an anthology of masterpieces."

Release date: May, 1976

CAST

Fred Astaire . . . . Himself
Gene Kelly . . . . Himself

CREDITS

New sequences directed by: Gene Kelly *Producers:* Saul Chaplin, David Melnick *Narration written by:* Leonard Gershe *Music arranged and conducted by:* Nelson Riddle *Special lyrics by:* Howard Dietz, Saul Chaplin *Director of photography:* George Folsey *Editors:* Bud Friedgan, David Blewitt *Contributing editors:* David Bretherton, Peter C. Johnson. An M-G-M presentation, released by United Artists. *Running time:* 133 minutes.

SYNOPSIS

1

"That's Entertainment," *The Band Wagon,* Fred Astaire, Nanette Fabray, Oscar Levant, Jack Buchanan; "That's Entertainment," *That's Entertainment, Part 2,* Fred Astaire, Gene Kelly; "For Me and My Gal," *For Me and My Gal,* Judy Garland, Gene Kelly; "Fascinating Rhythm," *Lady, Be Good,* Eleanor Powell; "I've Got a Feeling You're Fooling," *Broadway Melody of 1936,* Robert Taylor, June Knight; "La Chica Chaca," *Two Faced Woman,* Greta Garbo; "I Wanna Be a Dancin' Man," *The Belle of New York,* Fred Astaire; "Hi-Lilli, Hi-Lo," *Lili,* Leslie Caron; "Be a Clown," *The Pirate,* Judy Garland, Gene Kelly.

2

"Be a Clown," *That's Entertainment, Part 2,* Fred Astaire; "From This Moment On," *Kiss Me Kate,* Ann Miller, Tommy Rall, Carol Haney, Bobby Van, Bob Fosse, Jeanne Coyne; "All of You," *Silk Stockings,* Fred Astaire, Cyd Charisse; "Lonesome Polecat," *Seven Brides for Seven Brothers,* Howard Keel; "The Lady Is a Tramp," *Words and Music,* Lena Horne; "Smoke Gets in Your Eyes," *Lovely to Look At,* Kathryn Grayson, Gower and Marge Champion; "Easter Parade," *Easter Parade,* Fred Astaire, Judy Garland.

3

"Color Change," *That's Entertainment, Part 2,* Gene Kelly; "Temptation," *Going Hollywood,* Bing Crosby, Fifi D'Orsay; "Zing! Went the Strings of My Heart," *Listen, Darling,* Judy Garland; "Taking a Chance on Love," *Cabin in the Sky,* Ethel Waters, Eddie "Rochester" Anderson; "Swingin' the Jinx Away," *Born to Dance,* Eleanor Powell; "Stouthearted Men," *New Moon,* Nelson Eddy; "Lover Come Back to Me," *New Moon,* Jeanette MacDonald, Nelson Eddy; "Inka Dinka Doo," *Hollywood Party,* Jimmy Durante; "I Got Rhythm," *Girl Crazy,* Judy Garland, Mickey Rooney.

Fred Astaire and Gene Kelly.

4

"Be a Clown," *That's Entertainment, Part 2*, Gene Kelly; "Songwriters Revue of 1929," *Songwriters Revue*, Jack Benny; "Wedding of the Painted Doll," *The Broadway Melody*, original company; "O, Lady, Be Good," *Lady, Be Good*, Ann Sothern, Robert Young; "Broadway Serenade," *Broadway Serenade*, Lew Ayres, Al Shean; "For Every Lonely Heart," *Broadway Serenade*, Jeanette MacDonald; "Manhattan," *Words and Music*, Mickey Rooney, Tom Drake, Marshall Thompson; "Three Little Words," *Three Little Words*, Fred Astaire, Red Skelton; "Tales from the Vienna Woods," *The Great Waltz*, Fernand Gravet, Miliza Korjus.

5

"Shubert Alley," *That's Entertainment, Part 2*, Fred Astaire, Gene Kelly; "Good Morning," *Singing in the Rain*, Gene Kelly, Debbie Reynolds, Donald O'Connor; "Triplets," *The Band Wagon*, Fred Astaire, Nanette Fabray, Jack Buchanan; "Concerto in F," *An American in Paris*, Oscar Levant; "Have Yourself a Merry Little Christmas," *Meet Me in St. Louis*, Judy Garland, Margaret O'Brien; "Steppin' Out with My Baby," *Easter Parade*, Fred Astaire; "Ten Cents a Dance," *Love Me or Leave Me*, Doris Day; "I Got Rhythm," *An American in Paris*, Gene Kelly and kids; "The Tender Trap," *The Tender Trap*, Frank Sinatra; "Ol' Man River," *Till the Clouds Roll By*, Frank Sinatra; "I Fall in Love Too Easily," *Anchors Aweigh*, Frank Sinatra; "I Believe," *It Happened in Brooklyn*, Frank Sinatra, Jimmy Durante; "You're Sensational," *High Society*, Frank Sinatra, Grace Kelly; "I Begged Her," *Anchors Aweigh*, Frank Sinatra, Gene Kelly; "I'm Going to Maxim's," *The Merry Widow (1934)*, Maurice Chevalier; "Girls, Girls, Girls," *The Merry Widow (1934)*, Maurice Chevalier; "The Last Time I Saw Paris," *Till the Clouds Roll By*, Dinah Shore; "Our Love is Here to Stay," *An American in Paris*, Gene Kelly, Leslie Caron; "I'll Build a Stairway to Paradise," *An American in Paris*, Georges Guetary; "Can-Can," *The Merry Widow (1952)*, Gwen Verdon and dancers; "The Merry Widow Waltz," *The Merry Widow (1952)*, dancers.

6

"Cartoon Sequence," *That's Entertainment, Part 2*, Gene Kelly, Fred Astaire; "Sinbad the Sailor," *Invitation to the Dance*, Gene Kelly and cartoon figures; "Now You Has Jazz," *High Society*, Bing Crosby, Louis Armstrong; "A Couple of Swells," *Easter Parade*, Fred Astaire, Judy Garland; "Take Me to Broadway," *Small Town Girl*, Bobby Van; "Broadway Rhythm," *Singing in the Rain*, Gene Kelly, Cyd Charisse; "There's No Business Like Show Business," *Annie Get Your Gun*, Betty Hutton, Howard Keel; "I Like Myself," *It's Always Fair Weather*, Gene Kelly; "I Remember It Well," *Gigi*, Maurice Chevalier, Hermione Gingold; "Bouncin' the Blues," *The Barkleys of Broadway*, Fred Astaire, Ginger Rogers; "Water Ski Ballet," *Easy to Love*, Esther Williams; "That's Entertainment," *The Band Wagon*, Fred Astaire, Nanette Fabray, Oscar Levant, Jack Buchanan; and "Finale," *That's Entertainment, Part 2*, Fred Astaire, Gene Kelly.

Non-musical sequences from: *Adam's Rib*; *Bombshell*; *Boom Town*; *Boys Town*; *Bud Abbott and Lou Costello in Hollywood*; *China Seas*; *David Copperfield*; *A Day at the Races*; *Dinner at Eight*; *Gone with the Wind*; *Goodbye, Mr. Chips*; *Grand Hotel*; *Lassie Come Home*; *Laurel & Hardy's Laughing Twenties*; *Listen, Darling*; *A Night at the Opera*; *Ninotchka*; *Pat and Mike*; *The Philadelphia Story*; *Private Lives*; *Saratago*; *Strange Cargo*; *A Tale of Two Cities*; *Tarzan the Ape Man*; *The Thin Man*; *Two-Faced Woman*; *White Cargo*; *Without Love*; and *FitzPatrick "Traveltalks."*

Vincent Canby in the *New York Times*:
"*That's Entertainment, Part 2* is 99 7/10 percent pure magic. The three-tenths that aren't so great are the connectives between the film's individual sequences. Mostly, however, *Part 2* has been compiled with the kind of intelligence and affection that allow us to get some purchase on the Hollywood history made by M-G-M without spending our whole lives at

the job. The film is so studded with highlights that I suppose we should be grateful for the ordinary footage that is used to connect the old material. It gives us time to breathe."

Frank Rich in the *New York Post*:
"It's not easy to say discouraging words about a film that's as innocuous, innocent and well-intentioned as *That's Entertainment, Part 2.* If ever a movie was, in principle, critic-proof, *That's Entertainment, Part 2* is it . . . [it's]

significantly inferior to the earlier film; it has all of the first movie's weaknesses and few of its glories. Of course there have to be some high points, and there are: Ann Miller, Bobby Van and Bob Fosse ('I wonder whatever happened to him?' quips Kelly, ha ha) dancing to 'From This Moment On' from *Kiss Me Kate.* . . . Because the clips aren't presented in any particular order, there's no build in pitch and the movie seems to lose steam as it progresses."

"From This Moment On"

WON TON TON, THE DOG WHO SAVED HOLLYWOOD

Release date: May, 1976

CAST

Grayson Potchuck . . . . BRUCE DERN
Estie Del Ruth . . . . MADELINE KAHN
J. J. Fromberg . . . . ART CARNEY
Murray Fromberg . . . . PHIL SILVERS
Fluffy Peters . . . . TERI GARR
Rudy Montague . . . . RON LEIBMAN
Guest Stars (in order of appearance)
Tour guide . . . . Dennis Morgan
Tourist . . . . Shecky Greene
Dog catchers . . . . Phil Leeds, Cliff Norton
Short order cook . . . . Romo Vincent

Old man on bus	Sterling Holloway
Studio gatekeeper	William Demarest
Miss Battley	Virginia Mayo
Manny Farber	Henny Youngman
Philip Hart	Rory Calhoun
Assistant director	Billy Barty
Silent film director	Henry Wilcoxon
Silent film star	Ricardo Montalban
Stagehand 1	Jackie Coogan
Stubby Stebbins	Aldo Ray
Hedda Parsons	Ethel Merman
Cleaning woman	Yvonne De Carlo
Landlady	Joan Blondell
Priest in dog pound	Andy Devine
Special effects man	Broderick Crawford
Silent film star 2	Richard Arlen
Silent film villain	Jack La Rue
Visiting film star	Dorothy Lamour
Mrs. Fromberg	Nancy Walker
President's girl 1	Gloria De Haven
Radio interviewer	Louis Nye
Stagehand 2	Johnny Weissmuller
Dancing butler	Stepin Fetchit
Souvenir salesman	Ken Murray
Autograph hound	Rudy Vallee
Awards announcer	George Jessel
Rhoda Flaming	Rhonda Fleming
President's girl 2	*Ann Miller*
Paul Lavell	Dean Stockwell
James Crawford	Dick Haymes
David Hamilton	Tab Hunter
Richard Entwhistle	Robert Alda
Rudy's butler	Fritz Feld
President's girl 3	Janet Blair
Singing telegraph man	Dennis Day
Studio guard	Mike Mazurki
Cleaning women	The Ritz Brothers
Rudy's agent	Jesse White
Woman journalist	Carmel Myers
Male journalist	Jack Carter
Nick	Victor Mature
Nick's girl	Barbara Nichols
Premiere M.C.	Army Archerd
Premiere male star	Fernando Lamas
Premiere female star	Zsa Zsa Gabor
President's girl 4	Cyd Charisse
Moving man	Huntz Hall
Man in Mexican film	Doodles Weaver
Professor Quicksand	Edgar Bergen

Custard pie stars	Morey Amsterdam, Eddie Foy, Jr.
Slapstick star	Peter Lawford
Stars at screening	Patricia Morison, Guy Madison
Burlesque stagehand	Regis Toomey
Secretary at gate	Alice Faye
Grayson's studio secretary	Ann Rutherford
Blind man	Milton Berle
Drunk	John Carradine
Cook in kitchen	Keye Luke
Grayson's butler	Walter Pidgeon

BITS

Man on bus William Benedict *Old woman on bus* Dorothy Gulliver *Tailor* Eli Mintz *Second butler* Edward Ashley *Girl in Arab film* Kres Mersky *Waitress* Jane Connell *Fluffy's escort* Jack Bernardi *Mexican projectionist* Pedro Gonzales-Gonzales *Prostitute's customer* Eddie Le Veque *Mark Bennett* Ronny Graham *Priest* James E. Brodhead
And
WON TON TON ....
AUGUSTUS VON SCHUMACHER

CREDITS

Director: Michael Winner *Producers:* David V. Picker, Arnold Schulman, Michael Winner *Written by:* Arnold Schulman, Cy Howard *Director of photography:* Richard H. Kline, A.S.C. *Music by:* Neal Hefti *Associate producer/Unit production manager:* Tim Zinnemann *Art director:* Ward Preston *Set decorator:* Ned Parsons *Assistant director:* Charles Okun *2nd assistant director:* Arne Schmidt *Sound editor:* Terence Rawlings *Sound recording:* Bob Post *Re-recording mixer:* Hugh

With Art Carney.

Billy Barty, Jack Bernardi, Teri Garr, Phil Silvers, Bruce Dern,
Ann, Art Carney, and Won Ton Ton.

Strain *Auditor:* Gene Levy *Transportation captain:* James Brubaker *Makeup:* Philip Rhodes *Hair stylist:* Billie Laughridge *Assistant to Mr. Picker:* Laurence Mark *Assistant to Mr. Winner:* John Smallcombe *Dogs furnished by:* Lou Schumacher *Dogs trained by:* Karl Miller *Film editor:* Bernard Gribble *Running time:* 92 minutes.

MUSIC

"Paramount on Parade" by J. King and E. Janis; "Love Theme" from *The Godfather* by Nino Rota; "Hapy Birthday to You" by M. J. Hill and P. S. Hill; "Dagger-Dance" from *Natoma* by Victor Herbert.

SYNOPSIS

On the way to an audition in Hollywood in 1924, aspiring actress Estie Del Ruth (Madeline Kahn) meets Won Ton Ton, who falls in love with her and follows her.

J. J. Fromberg (Art Carney), head of New Era Studios, is evading bill collectors. Fromberg is broke and the studio is collapsing.

Estie gets an audition. Won Ton Ton saves her from a fate worse than death when the "director" turns out to be an electrician on the make. Fromberg sees the dog as the savior for his ailing studio. Grayson Potchuk (Bruce Dern) claims to own Won Ton Ton. Potchuk has been a tour-bus driver but he really wants to be a producer.

Won Ton Ton becomes a legendary star. Grayson becomes a producer, Estie the dog's trainer, and Fromberg the most successful studio head in Hollywood.

Leading man Rudy Montague (Ron Leibman) is then co-starred with Won Ton Ton. The results are disastrous for the dog, and the three are fired. But later Estie does become a star, and Potchuk and Fromberg learn the Hollywood tradition—one minute you're up, the next minute you're down.

CRITICAL REACTION

Richard Eder in the *New York Times:*
"What saves the movie, a jumble of good jokes and bad, sloppiness, chaos and apparently any old thing that came to hand, is Madeline Kahn. The movie itself is an untidy, somewhat pleasant mess, a string of sight and situation gags strung along a minimal plot about film-making in Hollywood of the 1920's. Bruce Dern is adequate as the young director. Art Carney's horrendous studio president is funny for a while. The dog is all right. But Miss Kahn upstages him. It is because of her that *Won Ton Ton* is something more than a dog."

Frank Rich in the *New York Post:*
"*Won Ton Ton, the Dog Who Saved Hollywood*, a dog of a movie now at showcase theaters, is a ragtag collection of crudely shot slapstick footage. It's a bone-crunching bore. The cast includes Bruce Dern, Madeline Kahn, Art Carney and Ron Leibman—they're all awful. There are also dozens of cameo appearances by famous and not-so-famous Hollywood actors of yesteryear, many of whom I had long since assumed to be dead; since the average cameo is a split-second in duration, however, it's impossible to say for sure who in the cast is or is not among the living. At one point, Won Ton Ton empties his bladder on one of his co-stars. What Won Ton Ton does to Carney is exactly what *Won Ton Ton, the Dog Who Saved Hollywood* does to its audience."

Madeline Kahn, Bruce Dern, and Won Ton Ton.

THE THEATER AND TELEVISION

George White had not mounted a production of his *Scandals* for four years when he decided to do a version in 1939. Since RKO had not picked up Ann Miller's contract, this was just the time she was looking to do a Broadway show. She knew it would boost her stock as a motion picture property.

In his revues White always featured the top stars available, together with gorgeous showgirls, and new talent. Although Ann was not unknown and had achieved some reputation from the RKO films and musicals she had appeared in, *Scandals* would be her Broadway debut.

"I got a chance to go into George White's *Scandals*," Ann said. "I had a good part. I danced, I sang, and I appeared in several of the skits. I certainly was happy while the show was being tried out in Boston and places like that.

"But the show had to be shortened and somehow I was involved in all the cuts. By the time we reached New York all I had to do was a couple of dance numbers. I wept. I begged Mr. White to let me quit, but he wouldn't do it."

The *Scandals* was exactly that—scandalous, with showgirls wearing provocative costumes, and with risque skits provided by Ben Blue, Willie and Eugene Howard, and The Three Stooges—all masters of broad burlesque humor. The Boston censors were alarmed at the blue material in the *Scandals* during the show's out-of-town tryout period, but the city was well-known for its puritanical atmosphere.

In contrast, the New York critics generally applauded the show and threw their hats in the air over Ann's performance. She was truly the discovery of the season. She stopped the show with her dance number in the first act, "The Mexiconga" (which White hoped would become as popular as "The Black Bottom," a number he had also introduced) and her solo turn in the second act.

"As it happened," Ann remembered, "New Yorkers were crazy about the Conga. And I had figured out a Conga tap dance. So on that first night the audience liked what I did. I know it sounds immodest to say so, but some of the people actually stood up and cheered." (Standing ovations, which today are commonplace, were rare then.)

The *Scandals* had a successful run at the Alvin Theater in New York (shows didn't have to run years to be hits at that time) and then proved to be a successful draw on tour for a year in such cities as Detroit, San Francisco, and Los Angeles. So, the *Scandals* did exactly what Ann and her agents had hoped it would do. Movie offers were made to Ann, and RKO, the highest bidder, again signed her for a picture. If Ann had not opted to return to California and the movies, it is quite certain that she would have become a major Broadway musical star. But New York would have to wait thirty years before Ann would be back in a Broadway musical, although in the interim she made in-person appearances in movie theaters to promote her film musicals.

The Hollywood studio system had become a white elephant by the late 1950s. It was the end of the Golden Era of the movie musical, and after Ann left M-G-M she made her television debut October 6, 1957, on Bob Hope's NBC comedy special. The show was filmed at Nouasseur Air Base in North Africa. Eddie Fisher, Gary Crosby, and Marie McDonald were also in the cast. Besides reprising "Too Darn Hot," her number from *Kiss Me Kate*, Ann appeared with Hope and Fisher in a sketch about a sheik. She next appeared as a guest with Dinah Shore and Patti Page on their network shows.

Ann's marriage to Texas oilman William Moss, on August 22, 1958, in La Jolla, California, caught her close friends offguard. Moss, who resembled Ann's first husband, Reese Milner, had been married to actress Jane Withers. Ann was on the rebound from attorney William V. O'Connor, whom everyone thought would be her next husband. Ann has said that O'Connor was the only true love in her life. But O'Connor was a divorced Catholic who couldn't remarry. The church would never recognize another marriage, since he had been married in the Catholic church, unless his former wife died. However O'Connor's former wife, Adele, married Lord Beatty in London.

Moss commuted regularly between Texas and California. Ann was expected to entertain lavishly and travel with her husband but soon found that she couldn't keep up with the hectic social pace and drinking parties.

"That marriage was doomed from the start," Ann recalls. Although the stormy union ended in May, 1961, Moss remains a good friend to this day.

With Dinah Shore on "Dinah's Place."   With Burl Ives on "The Hollywood Palace."

Even though she gave up her career each time she was married, Ann managed to appear on "The Perry Como Show" in 1959 and "The Ed Sullivan Show" in 1960.

Shortly after Ann's divorce from Moss, she married Arthur Cameron, whom she had known for twenty years. Cameron, another Texas oil millionaire, was much older than Ann. During a visit to Mexico City, Ann and Cameron were married on May 25, 1961. They separated on March 7, 1962. When Ann asked for a divorce, she was appalled. Cameron claimed that there had never been a legal ceremony!

The *Los Angeles Times*, on April 5, 1962,. in bold front-page head-lines, bannered Ann's lawsuit for $7,150,000 claiming Cameron had induced her into a fraudulent marriage. Cameron's lawyers contended that it was nothing more than an attempted suit for breach of promise. The court "annulled" the marriage.

Two years later, after appearing on "The Regis Philbin Show," Ann made her first appearance on "The Hollywood Palace," one of the top variety shows on television. Her first appearance was on December 12, 1964. The act cost approximately eight thousand dollars and she rehearsed for two months. The next Palace show she did was on May 22, 1965. Ann danced with Dante de Paulo to the song "Bill Bailey."

"This is one television show I really enjoy doing," Ann said in an interview in the *Los Angeles Herald-Examiner* "They know how to treat a star correctly on the 'Hollywood Palace.' I think that's half the reason people like the show—you can tell the stage is loaded with happy entertainers who feel they are being presented properly."

For her third appearance, on March 11, 1967, her big number, "Caught in the Web of Love," was taped as something like an M-G-M musical spectacular.

"I've been on programs where they never move a camera to follow the dancer, or take pains to have a good sounding-board for the taps. The 'Palace' is what we call a 'first-class house,' and I'm glad to see the ratings agree."

For her fourth appearance on "The Hollywood Palace," Ann performed "Slap that Bass" with four male dancers.

Ann has been on almost all the television talk shows—"Girl Talk," "The Tonight Show," "The Mike Douglas Show," with David Frost and Dick Cavett, and, most frequently, "The Merv Griffin Show." She has also made appearances on "Hollywood 65," "What's My Line?," "The Jonathan Winters Show," "Hollywood Squares," "The Dean Martin Show," and "The Arthur Murray Dance Party." On the "Bell Telephone Hour" aired March 13, 1966, Ann performed "I'm a Latin from Manhattan" and, paired with Ray Bolger, did "Puttin' on the Ritz."

A stock production of *Can-Can* in Houston proved to be Ann's stepping-stone back to Broadway. It was her first "book" show and one in which she had a lot of singing to do. The Cole Porter musical easily showcased Ann's talent, and reviewers praised her performance. In order to provide Ann with an opportunity to tap dance, a number was interpolated and she tapped on the judge's bench in the courtroom scene.

John Bowab, the associate producer of *Mame*, saw *Can-Can* in Houston and thought Ann would be a perfect choice for a Florida production of *Mame* that he was putting together with Jerry Herman.

Bowab's casting was ideal. Ann played to SRO houses in Miami, Palm Beach, and Fort Lauderdale for six weeks, and the audiences responded with standing ovations at every performance.

Mame, personified by Ann Miller, was given a much needed shot in the arm. (The Broadway show was on "two-fers," and business, though not bad, was less than capacity.) It was rumored that the show would close soon. But Ann's presence managed to turn the show around and box-office business was brisk.

Mame was ending its third year, and the current star, Jane Morgan, would soon be leaving the show. Ann, with the success of the Florida run of the musical, was signed to become the next "Mame," and opened at the Winter Garden Theater on May 26, 1969. Director Gene Saks had again polished the show, and Onna White choreographed the new tap section added to the "That's How Young I Feel" number in the second act.

On opening night she was radiant. The audiences went wild at her first entrance, and the frenzy continued throughout the show. Long lines of fans, many of them young and only recently aware of Ann's talents, waited after every performance at the stage door to see her. She graciously and patiently signed autographs and talked to as many people as her time and energy would allow.

Ann kept the musical going strong until January, 1970, when she contracted flu and pneumonia and *Mame* finally closed.

In 1971, a one-minute television commercial to promote Heinz's

Ann's fabulous soup commercial.

Great American Soups was produced and directed by Stan Freberg in the tradition of a 1937 Hollywood musical. The commercial was an extravaganza that took four weeks to complete. Ann Miller rose out of the ground, tapping on top of an eight-foot-high cylinder, backed by a twenty-four-piece orchestra, a bevy of chorines, and a twenty-foot-high "Dancing Waters" special effect.

Conductor Billy May scored the music, choreographer Hermes Pan devised the dance, Jack Poplin served as art director, and *Patton* camera-man Fred Koenekamp filmed the commercial on the Samuel Goldwyn soundstages. Dave Willock was seen briefly as Ann's husband. The cost? It was reported to have been $154,000, with the sponsor paying approximately $50,000 each time the spot was aired.

Dames at Sea, a "Bell System Family Theatre Special," followed on NBC on November 15, 1971. This television adaptation of the hit off-Broadway musical, which spoofed the Hollywood musicals of the thirties, starred Ann-Margret, Ann Miller, Anne Meara, Harvey Evans, Fred Gwynne, and Dick Shawn.

Ann, portraying Broadway star Mona Kent, did an exciting tap number, "Wall Street." "They cut twenty-four bars out of my opening number because they had a time problem. That really upset me be-

In a pensive mood in her New York
hotel suite overlooking Central Park.

cause that number could have been sensational," Ann said. "They cut
out another number completely because they thought that my part was
a little bit too strong for Ann-Margret's sake. That's the way to protect
a star."

Nevertheless, "Wall Street" was sensational, and Ann got the best
reviews when the special was aired. *Variety* noted, "Ann Miller stood
out for looks and otherwise as the temperamental star." John J. O'Connor wrote in the *New York Times:* "The show was not without its
moments, particularly when Ann Miller was allowed to tap out her
brassy impersonation of the temperamental star, Mona Kent." And Bob
Williams reported in the *New York Post* that "it all worked well in our
tiny viewing room, particularly with the presence of Ann Miller, who
really carried it, with her agelessly agile and attractive female frame."

On November 15, 1972, Ann appeared in the ABC-TV hit series
"Love, American Style." She later appeared on "Dinah's Place" on
NBC and with Charles "Buddy" Rogers and Rosemary Clooney on
March 30, 1974, in "Grammy Salutes Oscar" on CBS. Other TV spe-
cials in which she appeared were "The Magic of Christmas" with How-
ard Keel and the "Pre-Academy Awards Show" with Ricardo Montalban.

In recent years Ann has toured in stock productions of musical
classics such as *Anything Goes* and *Panama Hattie,* and revivals of

Mame and *Hello, Dolly*. Although some movie stars cannot bridge the gap from film work to the stage, Ann has taken gracefully to live theater. Her early stage experience gave her a good foundation for such a transition.

During the opening performance of *Anything Goes* at the St. Louis Municipal Opera, Ann was struck by the sliding steel curtain and suffered an injury to her inner ear. She spent more than four weeks in the hospital, and it was uncertain whether she would be able to dance again. Fortunately, after two years of having to walk with assistance, Ann recovered. Her lawsuit against the Muny Opera was settled out of court.

In 1977 and 1978 Ann appeared in New York as part of the Milliken Breakfast Show at the Waldorf-Astoria's Grand Ballroom. The famous industrial show, which costs more than a million dollars to produce, is one of the toughest tickets to come by in New York. The show rivals the best of Broadway and the performers are pampered, pleased, and treated royally.

"M-G-M rises again for one hour in a Milliken show!" Ann remarked. The producers of the opulent industrial show presented Ann with a 52 carat amethyst and diamond ring in appreciation for her work in which she stopped the show at every performance.

Martin Gottfried wrote in the *New York Post:* "The spirit surrounding this year's Milliken is especially nice, even to the point where Ann Miller could practically kid herself. Miss Miller was given the number you wanted most to see her do, with a tap-dancing chorus and a

Ann is a Broadway star! *Mame* at the
Winter Garden Theater, New York.

staircase for an entrance. Between her extraordinary hair, her gold sequin tights, the 'Ridin' High' music and her tap shoes, there was little more to ask of her."

After a tour of some fifty weeks during the 1978–79 season in *Cactus Flower*—in which Ann inserted a tap number to huge success—producer Harry Rigby, who had wanted to mount a Broadway revival of *Anything Goes* for Ann, finally signed her to co-star with Mickey Rooney in a new musical burlesque entitled *Sugar Babies*.

The show opened at the Curran Theater in San Francisco on May 13, 1979, to both critical and audience acclaim. After try-outs in Los Angeles, Chicago, Detroit, and Philadelphia, it opened at the Mark Hellinger Theater in New York on October 8, 1979. Except for one dissenter (Douglas Watt in the *Daily News*), all the newspaper and television critics praised the show and the two stars, Mickey Rooney and Ann Miller, and *Sugar Babies* became a Broadway smash hit.

And so, in a career spanning more than four decades, and one that shows no signs of diminishing as we enter the 1980's, the talents of Ann Miller, whether dancing in an extravagant M-G-M musical, in a Broadway show, or on a television special, have brought joy to theatergoers the world over.

For me, knowing Ann as a friend and working with her on a professional level, the experience has been a special one—lovely, pleasurable and exciting. It is a privilege to know Ann Miller.

As Patrick Dennis said to his Auntie Mame when he realized the joy and love she had brought into his life:

"Thank you, Moon Lady."

With Mickey Rooney.

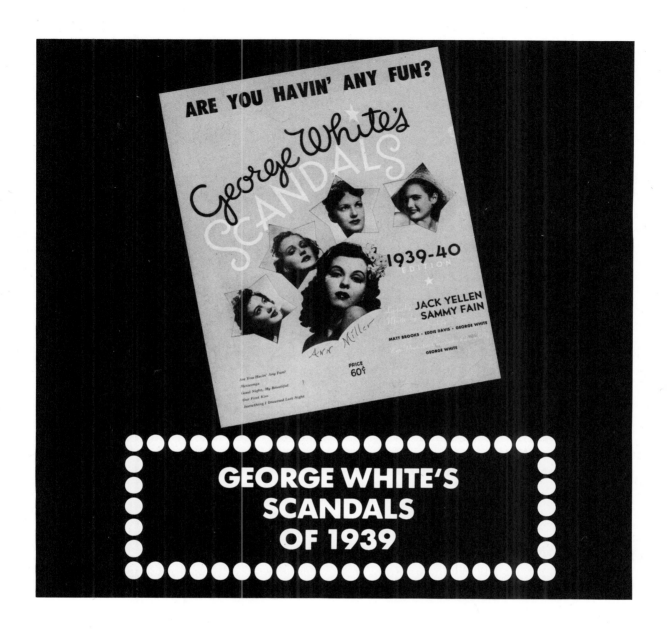

GEORGE WHITE'S SCANDALS OF 1939

ALVIN THEATER, NEW YORK

Opened August 28, 1939—closed December 9, 1939

CAST

WILLIE and EUGENE HOWARD, THE THREE STOOGES, BEN BLUE, ELLA LOGAN, ANN MILLER, RAYMOND MIDDLETON, ROSS WYSE, JR., JUNE MANN, BILLY RAYES, JACK WILLIAMS, COLLETTE LYONS, KIM LOO SISTERS, KNIGHT SISTERS, BETTY ALLEN, CRAIG MATHUES, LOIS ANDREW, HAROLD WHALEN, and Fred MANATT, Harry STOCKWELL, Martha Burnett, Christine FORSYTHE, Victor ARDEN and His Orchestra, and The George White Girls

CREDITS

Entire production conceived and staged by George White. Lyrics by Jack Yellin. Music by Sammy Fain. Dialogue by Matt Brooks, Eddie Davis and George White. Scenery designed by Albert Johnson. Costumes designed by Charles LeMaire, executed by Mme. Berthe. All fabrics by Dazians, Inc. Consultants on production, Max Weldy and Emil Friedlander. Dances by George White. Dialogue directed by William K. Wells. Additional lyrics by Herb Magidson. Orchestra conducted by Charles Drury. Orchestrations by Hans Spialek, Don Walker, Lew Harris and Ted Royal.

SYNOPSIS

ACT I

Overture—Victor Arden and His Orchestra (Victor Arden and Phil Wall at the Pianos)

1

"Scandals Day at the Fair": *Graves Whalen:* Raymond Middleton *Mayor La Guardia:* Ross Wyse, Jr. *Sam Taylor:* Willie Howard *Max Perisphere:* Eugene Howard *Lady from Havana:* Dorothy Koster *Amazon:* Florette DuElk *Lady in Ice:* Frances Neal *Dove Lady:* Rose Marie Magrill *And the George White Girls:* Barbara Lenton, Lois Andrew, Betty Allen, Christine Forsythe, Dorothy Stanton, Marie Kelly, Lois Hunt, Bonnie Bennett, Lillian Walsh, Florette DuElk, Miriam Franklin, Jane Hatfield, Dorothy Koster, Rhoda Long, Amy Collins, Fay Renault, Peggy Graham, Ginger Johnson, Jane Dixon, Fran English, Olga Gorey, Peggy Kirk, Georgia Jarvis, Mary King, Phyllis Dawn, Kay Buckley, Frances Neal, Loretta Kane, Marie Brady, Myra Weldon, Ella Windell, Constance Snow, Marji Beeler, Mary Carroll, Cece Ames, Mary Francis, Amelia Gentry, Prudence Hayes, Rose Marie Magrill, Betty Nielson, Lois Palmer, Dorothy Reed, Paula Rudolph, Gloria Scott, Helen Wishart, Mae Britton, Susan Carewe, June Curtis

2

"Theatre Quiz": *Professor Quiz:* Billy Rayes "Quiz No. 1" *Woman:* June Mann *Man:* Craig Mathues "Quiz No. 2" *Man:* James French "Quiz No. 3" *Boy:* Craig Mathues *Girl:* June Mann "Quiz No. 4" *Boy:* Billy Raye *Friend:* Craig Mathues "Quiz No. 5" *Man:* Craig Mathues *Girl:* June Mann

3

"Are You Having Any Fun?": Sung by Ella Logan, Kim Loo Sisters, The Three Stooges and the Girls

4

"Tel-U-Vision": *Business man:* Willie Howard *Salesman:* Eugene Howard *The Wife:* Collette Lyons *The Friend:* Harold Whalen *Iceman:* James French

5

"A Hat Like That": Sung by Ann Miller and Jack Williams

6

"The Stand In": *Bawdry:* Larry Fine *Director:* Moe Howard *The Stand In:* Curley Howard *Mexican Pete:* Raymond Middleton

7

"Smart Little Girls": Sung by Betty Allen, Lois Andrew, Vera Shea and Dorothy Koster, Kay Buckley, Rose Marie Magrill, Florence DuElk, Barbara Lenton and Amelia Gentry *Three Smart Girls* Sung by Moe Howard, Curley Howard and Larry Fine

8

"Yokel Boy": *Barker:* Harold Whalen *Yokel boy:* Ben Blue *Hostess:* Collette Lyons

9

"Our First Kiss": Sung by Craig Mathues, Lois Andrew and the Girls

10

"Columnist at Home": *Mrs. Winchell:* Collette Lyons *Walter Winchell:* Willie Howard *Maid:* June Mann

11

"The Mexiconga": Sung by Ella Logan and the Girls, and Ann Miller and The Kim Loo Sisters

12

"Curb Your Dog": Willie Howard, The Three Stooges, Lois Andrew and Dorothy Koster, Kay Buckley, Barbara Lenton and Frances Neal

13

Ross Wyse, Jr., and June Mann

14

"Tin Pan Alley": *Song plugger:* Raymond

"The Mexiconga"

Middleton *Music teacher*: Ella Logan *Customer*: Willie Howard *"My Old Kentucky Home"*: Martha Burnett *"Old Man River"*: Craig Mathues and the Girls and Entire Company

ENTR'ACT Victor Arden and His Orchestra

ACT II
1
"Good Night, My Beautiful": Sung by Harry Stockwell and Martha Burnett, and danced by the Girls and Knight Sisters
2
"Get It Wholesale": *Sam Zucker*: Eugene Howard *Willie Winn*: Willie Howard
3
Ann Miller
4
"Madame DuBarry": *Madame DuBarry*: Collette Lyons *Maid*: Betty Allen *Robert Taylor*: Moe Howard *Tyrone Power*: Larry Fine *Walt Disney*: Curley Howard
5
"In Waikiki": Sung by Ella Logan and danced by Christine Forsythe and the Girls

6
"Harvest Moon Winners": *Jitterbugs*: Betty Allen and Lois Andrew *Minuet*: Ben Blue, Collette Lyons and Harold Whalen
7
"There Must Be a Union": *Mrs. Murphy*: Betty Allen *Mr. Murphy*: Willie Howard *John L. Lewis*: Eugene Howard *Policeman*: Frederick B. Manatt
8
Billy Rayes
9
"Good Night, My Beautiful": As Gypsy Rose Lee Would Present It
10
The Three Stooges (Moe Howard, Curley Howard, Larry Fine)
11
"The Songs For Free": Ella Logan and Entire Company

CRITICAL REACTION

Variety:
"The vogue of costly revues passed out some seasons ago, and it was not expected that

George White, in returning from the Coast to Broadway, would present a production on a par with the previous *Scandals*. Show goes in for talent, is well-dressed, and has some standard tunes, distinctly rough comedy, but withal should do well. 'The Mexiconga,' touted as a standout and something new in stepping, staged by White, served more to show off Ann Miller, the finest girl tap dancer seen on Broadway boards in many seasons. Coast brunet beauty, displaying her supple legs, is easily the show's individual hit, house going for her in a big way. Miss Miller's exhibition of multiple tapping in the second part was a further bid for popularity."

Robert Coleman in the
New York Daily Mirror:

"It's swell for the grown ups, but we suggest that you keep the kiddies on their birds and bees texts. For it would be a too wise child who sees *Scandals*. And now to the dance. White introduces, in Ann Miller, the greatest gal tapster to hit Broadway since Eleanor Powell went to Hollywood. Ann is terrific. She's an eye tonic, has loads of style and a personality that whirls with hurricane force across the footlights. The 1939 *Scandals*, in sum, is a cavalcade of laughs, tunes and beauties."

Richard Manson in the *New York Post*:

"Mr. White's latest effort, while it has its melodious and amusing intervals, is still a shadow of *Scandals* glory. Ella Logan handles most of the vocal assignment and is as cute as a new penny. She's also the shining light in 'Mexiconga,' the most colorful item in the whole production. Ann Miller, a recruit from the cinema, does the stepping in this and stops the show. Mr. White can take a bow for this bundle of rhythm—she has the talent, the figure and the assurance for big things."

Burns Mantle in the
New York Daily News:

"I would not say that George White is back in top form with *Scandals*—his touch is a little heavy in this 1939 revival and he lists rather heavily to the burlesque side. The cheaper burlesque side. He has picked the girls with care as he usually does; he has spent a lot of money on costumes and has hunted out a new entertainer or two to lend a touch of freshness to several of the numbers. The new faces include Ann Miller, a shapely tap dancer with a talent that is exceptional and a pictorial appeal beyond that of many of her tapping sisters."

Brooks Atkinson in the
New York Times:

"In case business men get tired this year, George White has thoughtfully provided a haven for them with a new *Scandals* which opened at the Alvin last evening. According to the formula that served him in the golden age, he has assembled the usual virtues and vices in a swiftly paced review. The virtues include a chorus worth looking at, a song or two that rises above mediocrity, a heat-treated dance called 'The Mexiconga'—Ann Miller can tap dance with virtuosity. After an absence of four years, Mr. White has come back with an average *Scandals*—good looking, fleet and dirty."

Lucius Beebe in the
New York Herald Tribune:

"The thirteenth edition of the *Scandals* has a great deal to recommend it. To an embattled audience of George White enthusiasts there were many other attractions, among the most notable of whom were Miss Ann Miller, who scattered sex and sequins around the premises in a manner provocative of vast leering and applause. The current *Scandals* is a generous and gusty business . . . taken, to coin a phrase, all in all, the *Scandals* is fast, handsome, noisy and at times hilarious stuff.

George Ross in the
New York World Telegram:

"Let no one say that the current *Scandals* is short on that staple commodity, sex appeal —coupled with talent. There's Ann Miller of Hollywood, whose trim torso and nimble tap-dancing stopped the show at one point and lifted it up at another."

John Anderson in the
New York Journal American:
"The new *Scandals* exhibited the standard White equipment with a 1939 label. 'The Mexiconga,' offered as a sequel to the Black Bottom, simply isn't, though Ann Miller dances it and other tap numbers with relentless precision."

Richard Lockridge in the *New York Sun:*
"The new *Scandals* is, at intervals, about as coarse a show as a producer could reasonably expect to get by with. Ann Miller, wearing some of Mr. LeMaire's most provocative costumes, dances effortlessly and stops the show."

Arthur Pollock in the
Brooklyn Daily Eagle:
"Mr. White's latest *Scandals* is as scandalous as anything he has ever done. Mr. White, who brought the world the Black Bottom and other dance eccentricities now has something he calls 'The Mexiconga'—and Ann Miller taps in a way that will probably bring her fame."

A MUSICAL COMEDY IN
TWO ACTS AND SIXTEEN SCENES

At the Winter Garden Theatre, New York

CAST

Patrick Dennis, age 10	Chris HAGAN
Agnes Gooch	Helen GALLAGHER
Vera Charles	Anne FRANCINE
Mame Dennis	ANN MILLER
Ralph Devine	Henry Brunjes
Bishop	Casper Roos
M. Lindsay Woolsey	Ray MacDonnell
Ito	Sab Shimono

Doorman . . . . Art Matthews
Elevator boy . . . . Ross Miles
Messenger . . . . Jim Connor
Dwight Babcock . . . . Williard WATERMAN
Art model . . . . Jo Tract
Dance teacher . . . . Johanna Douglas
Leading man . . . . Casper Roos
Stage manager . . . . Art Matthews
Madame Branislowski . . . . Tally Brown
Gregor . . . . Jim Connor
Beauregard Jackson Picket Burnside . . . . Robert R. KAYE
Uncle Jeff . . . . Jim Connor
Cousin Fan . . . . Laurie Franks
Sally Cato . . . . Margaret Hall
Mother Burnside . . . . Tally Brown
Patrick Dennis, ages 19–29 . . . . David CHANEY
Junior Babcock . . . . Jerry Wyatt
Mrs. Upson . . . . Johanna Douglas
Mr. Upson . . . . John C. Becher
Gloria Upson . . . . Susan Walther
Pegeen Ryan . . . . Diane Coupe
Peter Dennis . . . . Chris HAGAN
Mame's friends . . . . Diana Baffa, Diane Blair,
    Ronald Bostick, Henry Brunjes, Eileen Casey, Jim Connor, Luigi
    Gasparinetti, Roland Ireland, Danny Joel, Art Matthews, Ross
    Miles, Eric Painter, Michael Misita, Carol Richards, Kathleen
    Robey, Mary Roche, Casper Roos, Bella Shalom, Jo Tract, Eleanor
    Treiber, Susan Walther, Jerry Wyatt.

CREDITS

Directed by Gene Saks. Produced by Sylvia and Joseph Harris, Robert Fryer, and Lawrence Carr. Book by Jerome Lawrence and Robert E. Lee. Music and lyrics by Jerry Herman. Based on the novel *Auntie Mame* by Patrick Dennis, and the play by Lawrence and Lee. Dances and musical numbers staged by Onna White. Associate producer, John Bowab. Settings designed by William and Jean Eckart. Costumes designed by Robert Mackintosh. Lighting by Tharon Musser. Musical direction and vocal arrangements by Donald Pippin. Orchestrations by Philip J. Lang. Dance music arranged by Roger Adams. Production musical director, Shepard Coleman. Assistant choreographer, Tom Panko. Hair styles by Ronald DeMann. Company manager, Richard Grayson. Production stage manager, Terrence Little. Stage managers, Ralph Linn and Paul Phillips. Dance captain, Diana Baffa. Miss Miller's and Miss Francine's costumes executed by Barbara Matera, Ltd. Costumes executed by Eaves Costume Company and Brooks-Van Horn Costume Company.

MUSICAL NUMBERS

"St. Bridget," "It's Today," "Open a New Window," "The Man in the Moon," "My Best Girl," "We Need a Little Christmas," "The Fox Hunt," "Mame," "Bosom Buddies," "Gooch's Song," "That's How Young I Feel," "If He Walked into My Life"

SYNOPSIS

Young Patrick Dennis (Chris Hagan) and his nanny, Agnes Gooch (Helen Gallagher) arrive at the New York home of his only living relative, Mame Dennis (Ann Miller), a rather eccentric and free-living person.

Mame is delighted at the prospect of having her own little boy to raise. Patrick's trustee, Dwight Babcock (Williard Waterman) wants the boy to attend an exclusive boys' school, but Mame decides to let life be his teacher.

The stock-market crash wipes out Mame's assets. Her best friend, actress Vera Charles (Anne Francine) gets Mame a part in her new show. But during the out-of-town tryout Mame ruins the show and is fired.

Next she becomes a manicurist at a very exclusive men's salon. Madame Branislowski (Tally Brown) and her assistant Gregor (Jim Connor) are horrified when she mangles the hand of a wealthy patron, Beauregard Jackson Pickett Burnside (Robert R. Kaye).

However, Beau is taken with Mame. When things at the Dennis household look their bleakest, Beau invites Mame to his plantation, Peckerwood. At the fox hunt, Mame not only catches the fox but wins the hearts of Beau and his relatives.

Time passes. Patrick (David Chaney), grown up, comforts "his best girl," Auntie Mame, when she becomes widowed. He also falls in love with snob Gloria Upson (Susan Walther). When Mame meets Gloria's parents (Johanna Douglas and John C. Becher), she discovers that they are bigots.

Mame tries to show Patrick that he is making a mistake, and at a party she gives for the Upsons he finally realizes that he has been wrong.

Patrick marries decorator Pegeen Ryan (Diane Coupe). Their son Peter (Chris Hagan) now gives Mame another little love to teach and to open new windows for.

CRITICAL REACTION

John Chapman in the *New York Sunday News:*

"There have been six Auntie Mames in the Winter Garden production of *Mame* since the musical opened in May, 1966. I saw the newest one, Ann Miller, the other night, and she is the best in my fond heart. Toward the end of the second act Miss Miller goes into a tap dance, which everybody has been waiting for —and it is indeed a dance. The audience I was with was warmly enthusiastic."

Clive Barnes in the *New York Times:*

"Ann Miller brings zest to *Mame*. She gives the show a real shot in the arm. Her legs are

better than ever and she dances superbly. If you haven't seen *Mame* before, it remains a Broadway must—and even if you have I think you may well find Miss Miller worth a detour."

Emory Lewis in the *Morning Call*:
"Spend another evening with Mame. She is indestructible, and you'll have a helluva good time. Ann Miller is the best dancer who has ever played the role. She gives the musical a delightful bounce it needs. She sings with distinction [and] she is a surprisingly good comedienne. She is as beautiful as ever, with legs that rival the celebrated Dietrich stems. Her face is curiously more beautiful now than when she was the Hollywood dance star. The party at Mame's is still one of the best parties in town. The lady is a perfect hostess."

Leonard Harris, CBS-TV:
"Ann Miller got a wild ovation before she began . . . and I must say she went on to justify it. She gives the part a dimension it never had before."

Douglas Watt in the *New York News*:
"Ann Miller stopped the show, time and again. She's charmingly alive and the happy owner of the most beautiful legs on Broadway. *Mame* benefits immeasureably from the presence of this lovely brunette."

William Mazlitt in the *Hollywood Reporter*:
"The applause for Ann Miller was unbelievable, the bravos never-ending, the whistles, the gee-whiz was overwhelming!"

Earl Wilson in the
New York Post:

"Ann Miller is a sensational smash in *Mame!* Her dancing legs, dancing thighs and dancing derriere are as overwhelming as her energy. [She] had the audience impersonating a yo-yo for numerous standing ovations. It's going to be Ann Miller's town for weeks."

Humm. in *Variety*:

"Fryer, Carr & Harris may have found a box-office stimulus for *Mame* in Ann Miller. Miss Miller is probably the best 'Mame' since Angela Lansbury, the original. Her singing voice is pleasant, her acting is authoritative and her dancing is excellent. She projects warmth and sincerity and works smoothly with the other performers. She looks smashing, with lovely black hair and an endearing smile, not to mention whistle-worthy legs. At the performance caught, [the tap number] aroused the audience to prolonged enthusiasm."

Marilyn Stasio in *Cue*:

"The current loopy lady of Beekman Place is the vivacious Ann Miller, looking absolutely sensational and obviously just busting to dance all over the stage. Miss Miller is blessed with that charismatic star 'something' that dominates the stage, and with the Miller presence buoying it, the show takes on the luster of life."

John J. O'Connor in the
Wall Street Journal:

"In *Mame*, Miss Miller finally steps into the leading actress category herself, and she is thoroughly delightful. Her acting is excellent, her sense of timing impeccable, and her singing of Jerry Herman's songs strong and pleasant. Most of all, of course, there is the Miller dancing, and here the actress has the audience cheering with every step—or even the hint of one. She brings a barrelful of zest to all of the numbers, but she stops the show with a special tap number added for her own particular talent. The cheers are partially wonderment, partially nostalgia, all deserved tribute. One of the most impressive things about Miss Miller's performance is the obvious lift it is giving to the rest of the cast. The mood is unmistakeably up at the Winter Garden Theater these evenings. There was some talk before Miss Miller arrived on the scene about the possibility of *Mame* finally closing. Nonsense. It's a brand new ballgame."

Winter Garden Theatre

PLAYBILL
the national magazine for theatregoers

MAME

TERRY ALLEN KRAMER AND HARRY RIGBY
in Association with Columbia Pictures present

SUGAR BABIES

THE BURLESQUE MUSICAL IN TWO ACTS

CAST

Mickey	MICKEY ROONEY
Scot	Scot STEWART
Jillian	Ann JILLIAN
Tom	Tom BOYD
Peter	Peter LEEDS
Jack	Jack FLETCHER
Jimmy	Jimmy MATHEWS
Ann	ANN MILLER
Sid	Sid STONE
The Sugar Babies	Chris Elia, Laura Booth,

Barbara Hanks, Robin Manus, Barbara Mandra, Diane Duncan,

Rose Scudder, Christine Busini, Debbie Gornay, Jeri Kansas, Linda
Ravinsky, Michele Rogers, Patti Watson, Faye Fujisaki Mar
The Male Ensemble . . . . Jonathan Aronson, Eddie Pruett,
Jeff Veazey, Michael Radigan
Swing dancers . . . . Hank Brunjes, Laurie Sloan
And: Bob WILLIAMS

CREDITS

Conceived by Ralph G. Allen and Harry Rigby. Sketches by Ralph G. Allen, based on traditional material. Music by Jimmy McHugh. Lyrics by Dorothy Fields, Harold Adamson, Al Dubin. Additional music and lyrics by Arthur Malvin. Associate producer, Jack Schlissel. Entire production supervised by Ernest Flatt. Sketches directed by Rudy Tronto. Staged and choreographed by Ernest Flatt. Scenery and costumes designed by Raoul Pene du Bois. Lighting designed by Gilbert V. Hemsley, Jr. Vocal arrangements by Arthur Malvin. Musical director, Glen Roven. Orchestrations by Dick Hyman. Dance music arranged by Arnold Gross. Associate producers, Thomas Walton Associates and Frank Montalvo. Hairstyles designed by Joseph Dal Corso. Company manager, Alan Wasser. Production stage manager,

"Don't Blame Me"

Christopher Kelly. Stage manager, Bob Burland. Assistant stage managers, Jay B. Jacobson, David Campbell. Assistant to Mr. Flatt, Toni Kaye. Doves trained by Ed Krieg.

SYNOPSIS

ACT I

1

Overture

2

A Memory of Burlesque
Song: "A Good Old Burlesque Show"—Mickey Rooney and his friends

3

Welcome to the Gaiety
Song: "Let Me Be Your Sugar Baby"—Peter Leeds, Jack Fletcher and The Sugar Babies

4

Meet Me 'Round the Corner—Jimmy Mathews, Scot Stewart, Peter, Mickey, Rose Scudder, Chris Elia, Michele Rogers and Ann Jillian

5

Travelin'
Songs: "In Louisiana," "I Feel a Song Comin' On," "Goin' Back to New Orleans"—Ann Miller, The Sugar Babies and The Gaiety Quartet

6

The Broken Arms Hotel—Jack, Tom Boyd, Mickey, Jimmy and Rose

7

Feathered Fantasy (Salute to Sally Rand)
Song: "Sally"—Scot, Barbara Hanks and The Sugar Babies

8

The Pitchman—Sid Stone

9

Ellis Island Lament
Song: "Immigration Rose"—Mickey and The Gaiety Quartet

10

Scenes from Domestic Life—Jillian, Jimmy, Jack, Peter, Tom, Scot, Robin Manus, Laura Booth and Debbie Gornay

11

Torch Song (Salute to Ed Wynn)
Song: "Don't Blame Me"—Ann and Eddie Pruett

12

Orientale—Christine Busini, introduced by Jack

13

The Little Red Schoolhouse—Ann, Rose, Diane Duncan, Jimmy and Mickey

14

The New Candy-Coated Craze
Song: "The Sugar Baby Bounce"—Jillian, Chris and Linda Ravinsky

15

Special Added Attraction: Madame Rentz and her All Female Minstrels featuring Countess Francine—Introduction by Jack
Songs: "Down at the Gaiety Burlesque," "Mr. Banjo Man"—Ann, Mickey, Jeff Veazey and The Sugar Babies

ACT II

1

Candy Butcher—Sid and The Gaiety Quartet

2

Girls and Garters
Songs: "I'm Keeping Myself Available for You," "Exactly Like You"—Jillian and The Sugar Babies

3

Justice Will Out—Tom, Peter, Mickey, Ann

4

In a Greek Garden (Salute to Rosita Royce)
Song: "Warm and Willing"—Jillian

5

Presenting Madame Alla Gazaza—Peter, Sid, Ann, Jeff, Mickey, Jimmy, Jack, Eddie, Jillian, Jonathan, Chris

6

Tropical Madness
Song: "Cuban Love Song"—Scot and Michele

7

Cautionary Tales—Rose, Jimmy, Eddie, Michael Radigan, Jeri Kansas, Jack, Peter, Tom and Sid

8

McHugh Medley
Songs: "Every Day Another Tune," "I Can't Give You Anything but Love, Baby," "I'm Shooting High," "When You and I Were Young, Maggie Blues," "On the Sunny Side of the Street"—Mickey and Ann

9

Presenting Bob Williams

10

Old Glory
Song: "You Can't Blame Your Uncle Sammy" —The Full Company

CRITICAL REACTION

Walter Kerr in the *New York Times*:
"Liked Miss Miller, too, in stunning shape at whatever age she must be, ready to leap from a baggage cart, whip off gloves and overskirt, and tap as though there'd been no yesterday. Strides through sketches, split-skirt put to good advantage, with a hammer-and-tongs authority, too. And I had a grand time, thank you."

Clive Barnes in the *New York Post*:
"With Mickey Rooney, the mighty atom, at his tumultuous best, and Ann Miller tip-tapping her way into second-stardom it should prove a sizeable Broadway hit. Still the Broadway belles are pretty and plentiful, Ann Miller pluckily looking like a frozen clone of her former self is spirited, and there are some neat old burlesque comics. The show is solidly on the shoulders of Broadway's most promising newcomer of the year. Rooney is the true icing on *Sugar Babies*."

Rex Reed in the *New York Daily News*:
"Mickey Rooney and Ann Miller knocked me senseless with their dazzle. They turned their new home at the Mark Hellinger Theatre into New Year's Eve on Times Square and sent show business soaring into orbit. I loved the fact that Mickey Rooney and Ann Miller have proved, once again, there's nothing like the old pros. Everyone and everything in *Sugar Babies* would make wonderful company for centuries to come. *Sugar Babies* is here to stay. I loved *Sugar Babies*."

Rick Talcove in the *Valley News*:
"With a super cast headed by Mickey Rooney and Ann Miller (two stars who still have surprises about them) *Sugar Babies* sets out to prove that an evening in the theater can consist of simply having fun. The show starts out like gangbusters and never lets up. Mickey Rooney is nothing less than phenomenal. And what can one say about Ann Miller? Yes, she still looks great and tap-tap-taps her heart out. But did you know Ms. Miller could belt out

With the male ensemble.

With Mickey Rooney.